The Great Arizona Adventure

Books by Eileen Moore

Arizona Trails for Children
Standing Watch: The Fire Towers of Arizona
Living with Fibromyalgia Rx Free
Coming 2020 - Living Springs in an Arid Land
Hiking Together

The natural world is not Disneyland where each encounter is carefully controlled. Before leaving home, we must anticipate and prepare for any changes in weather patterns and potential injury while exploring the natural world. The responsibility for safety while exploring Arizona remains with each individual. The author and all associated with this book, directly or indirectly, disclaim any liability for accidents, injuries, damages or losses which may occur when using this book. If you have any questions about exploring the outdoors, please consult the experts at the Forest Service, the Park Service and Arizona's Game and Fish Department.

The Great Arizona Adventure
Published by
Morten Moore Publishing
PO Box 881
Flagstaff, Az 86002

ISBN 978-0-9991108-4-3
Copyright 2018
All rights reserved
No part of this publication may be reproduced without written permission by Morten Moore Publishing.
Cover Photograph: Serenity Trujillo
All other photos by Eileen Moore except as designated.
Printing and Distribution by Ingram Spark

The Great Arizona Adventure

Contents

Dad, I Need an Adventure!   1

Caves   7

Sink Holes   18

Bridges & Arches   20

Mines   26

Volcanoes   31

Sand & Sandstone   42

Water   44

A Crack in the Earth   60

Green & Growing   64

Animals   71

Old Ruins   86

One Special Place   100

Gavin punched the button on his X-box controller and tossed it on the couch. Slumping down in his seat, he stared outside. This was hard to admit but he wanted to do something different! Something different than playing his video games. He would hate to admit that to his friends or to his mom. She was always telling him to go outside and play.

I need an adventure, he thought. He walked into the kitchen. His mom was not there.

He could hear his dad striking the keys on his keyboard at the computer in his office. He peered into the dim room.

"Dad, I need an adventure!"
"Humpf! An adventure?"
"Yeah, can we go on an adventure, Dad?"
His dad looked up from his computer.
"Why don't you go outside and play?"

"Why? I go outside all the time."

"We could go to the park," said his dad.

"No, Dad! I want a real adventure. You know being outdoors, going some place exciting. Maybe we could go camping."

"Camping? With the bears? With the mosquitos?" His dad did not seem to think this was a good idea.

"An adventure, Dad! I need an adventure!"

"What's going on?" asked Gavin's two older brothers as they walked into the room.

"Gavin says he needs an adventure."

"An adventure, huh? You are going to need some equipment if you're going on an adventure."

"Like what?" Gavin asked.

His brothers looked at each other.

Uh, oh! He knew that look and he was sure their idea might not be so good for him.

"You'll need a sleeping bag!"

His brother shoved a rolled bag into his chest. Gavin smiled.

"How about a tent?" The bag holding the tent landed on his lap.

"A pad to sleep on would be good." Another bag landed on Gavin.

"He needs a lantern," said his other brother.

"Don't break that glass!" said his dad. Gavin peered around the bag to see his dad smiling.

"He needs a flashlight to go with that lantern. Middle of the night, you want to see that bear knocking on your tent door!"

"Funny, Dad!" Gavin clutched the flashlight.

"If he is going to meet a bear, he better have a knife?" said his brother.

A knife dropped into Gavin's hand. Gavin stared at the knife. He had never been given a knife before.

His brother glared at him.

"You don't get to keep my knife, Gavin. This is just a loan for your big adventure!"

"Don't forget his hiking boots," said his mom.

Where had his mom come from? The boots landed on his lap.

"How about a compass?"

"How about a hat?"

"You'll need a water bottle."

"And a map!"

"Don't forget food," called his mom from the kitchen.

Food was good. He was almost afraid to look at how big the pile was getting!

"Wait a minute!" Gavin shoved the equipment to the floor.

"I don't want to carry all this stuff! Dad, when I said I wanted an adventure, I meant a small adventure."

"A small adventure? Just what did you have in mind?" asked his dad.

"I want to go exploring. I want to see some cool things."

"Like what, Gavin?"

"C'mon Dad, I'll show you! Let's go!"

No Windows!

No Lights!

Kind of spooky.

Somebody turn the lights on!

Gavin, you said you wanted an adventure!
This is a cave!

CAVES

"Gavin, caves are like dark rooms hidden underground. When you turn the lights out, it is dark! No windows, no holes in the cave ceiling to give us light from the outside. Caves can be very dark. That's why we carry flashlights so we can see where we are going."

"Can we go into the caves? Are there any bad guys down there? How about monsters? Are there monsters in caves?"

"One question at a time. Yes, we can go into some caves. There are no bad guys and no monsters in the caves. However, we might find a bear!"

"A bear? Really?"

"No, Gavin, I'm teasing you! Usually bears have dens hidden away in the forest. I don't think we will run into any bears."

"Dad, it's kind of spooky in some of these dark places. Do people ever hide stuff in caves? You know, like bandits hiding the money they stole."

"That's possible. Arizona history has a lot of stories about lost mines and stagecoach robberies. Seriously, I doubt you'll find any gold, Gavin, but we could find some other amazing things."

"Dad, are there there are lot of caves hidden under our feet? How are these caves made?"

"Gavin, most caves are created by water passing through cracks in the rock. Sometimes, the earth shifts and a crack appears. I know a cave that was created by rocks on fire. What do you think of that?"

"Dad, I don't think you can burn a rock. You're teasing me."

"No, Gavin! I'm serious. You said you wanted an adventure. Go find your flashlight. And you better get your pop-gun for those bears."

"Dad, you're teasing me."

"Yup. Let's go!"

"Gavin, before we get too far, we better look at a map of the places we are going to explore."

"A map? Dad, can't we just use the GPS on your phone like you do when we're going some place around town?"

"We can use technology to help us find a lot of places but sometimes a map gives us a better overview of the area we want to explore."

"So where are we on this map, dad?"

"You and I are standing in that yellow blob in the middle of the map. Do you see the names of other places on the map?"

"Yeah, I do. Are those towns in Arizona?"

"That's right. These are towns where people live. These people like adventures, too. They start in a different place but use the same map to find places they wish to explore."

"How do I know which direction I'm going on the map?"

"Just remember the top of the map is always north. If you check your compass, the little arrow will point north, too. First we find the spot where we are, then we can turn in the direction we want to go."

"Dad, let's look at the map each time we find something interesting so that I know where we are. OK?"

"What do you think about visiting a cave?"

"Sure, I'll get a flashlight."

"Then, let's check out some of Arizona's caves."

General Information on Arizona you may (or may not) want to know.

Arizona is not all desert! The Colorado plateau in northern Arizona rises to 7,000 feet in elevation. The mountains of Arizona stretch in the shape of an arc from the town of Williams east and south to the border with Mexico.

The Grand Canyon divides the northwest section of the state from the rest of Arizona. The land north of the Grand Canyon is called the Arizona strip.

Arizona's major rivers are the Colorado, Salt, Gila, Verde, Aqua Fria, Black, Blue and Virgin. Most of Arizona's lakes are reservoirs with the water held behind big dams.

Flagstaff averages 18 inches of precipitation while Phoenix receives 7 1/2 and Yuma a mere 3 1/4 inches each year.

Arizona has 20 reservations set aside for native American tribes.

Arizona became a state on February 14, 1912. It was previously part of the territory of New Mexico.

If you were to drive north from the Mexico border to the Arizona border with Utah, south to north across Arizona, at 65 miles per hour, the journey would take between seven to eight hours. Without stopping!

Gavin, before we get too far, we better look at a map of Arizona.

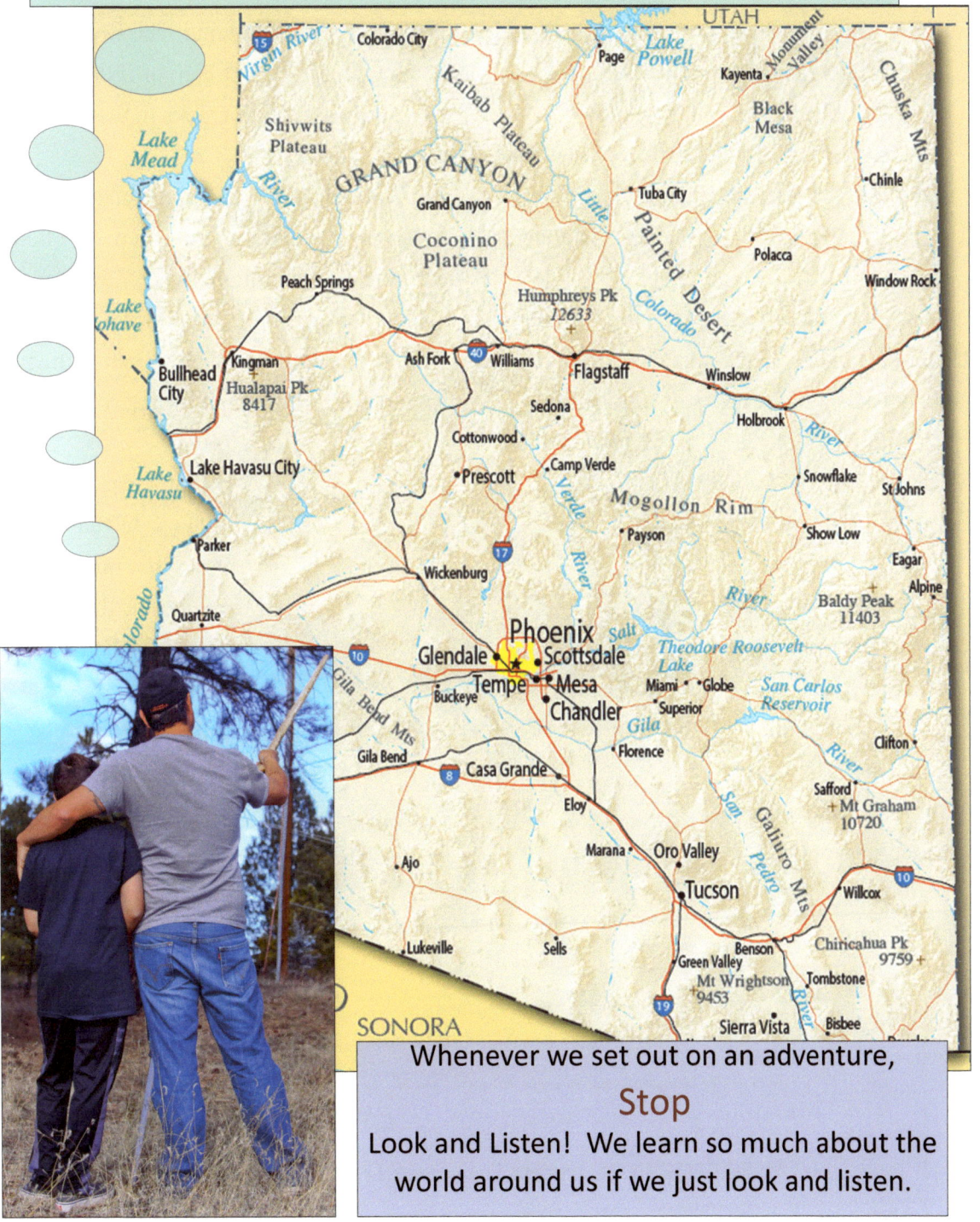

Whenever we set out on an adventure,

Stop

Look and Listen! We learn so much about the world around us if we just look and listen.

If a cave is a deep dark hole, how did the cave form under the surface of the earth?

Caves are carved out of rock by water, by chemical reactions and by the movement of the earth. As rain and snow descend onto the earth's surface, the water sinks into the ground. If the rock is limestone and the water seeping through the cracks is combined with carbon dioxide, it begins to dissolve the limestone formation. In sandstone, the water would carry away small grains of sand from the rock formations to form a cave. Other caves are formed when rocks collide or separate as the surface of the earth moves under pressure.

Regardless of the type of formation, little cracks become big cracks and may widen into rooms. Some rooms are as big as an arena.

Scientists describe a cave as *living* when water is present and creating rock formations. The water may be an underground stream or little drops of rain sliding through cracks in the rock, one drop at a time.

Water dripping through cracks in the rock may deposit minerals on a cave floor forming a rock column called a *stalagmite*. *Stalactites* are rock formations hanging from the ceiling of the cave. When the two join in one column, the formation is called a pillar.

Drip, drip, drip. These formations grow as the minerals in the water begin to harden along each column.

Stalagmites and stalactites are not the only formations in the cave. Some rocks appear to be the folds of a curtain, others look like popcorn. When you visit a cave, look around. What do you see in the rocks?

Can you imagine a lake hidden deep in a cave?

In some caves, the water collects in small pools while other caves have streams flowing through the open spaces. The Cave of the Bells in the Santa Rita Mountains has a pool of water that grows and shrinks with the seasons. Just don't plan on going swimming!

When the cave dries out, it is no longer described as a living cave. Caves are very fragile. In walking through them we introduce bacteria that is new to the cave and may begin to grow. The early explorers shoved over rock formations, left big, soggy foot prints and did a lot of damage. They did not have much equipment to explore these secret places. Some carried candles or lanterns to see their way. There were no pathways to follow. They had to use ropes to drop from one level to the next. So they made their own paths and sometimes damaged the caves. In time they began to bring other people into the caves, causing more damage.

They did not know they were harming the caves. Over time, we learn more about the world around us and our ideas change.

In November 1974, Gary Tenen and Randy Tufts found Karchner Cavern but they did not tell anyone until the State of Arizona agreed to protect the cave. You will learn more about our State Parks at the end of the book. If we are to protect our caves, we must all recognize that caves have a special life of their own.

Photo: NPS Gallery

Good news!
There are no vampire bats in Arizona. Vampire bats live in the Amazon basin in South America!

Arizona Game and Fish lists 28 species of bats in Arizona. What species of bat sucks nectar from the yucca agave plant?
  Look up the Lesser Long-nose and the Mexican Long-tongue bat. These nectar fans will even visit a hummingbird feeder for a sip of sugar water.

We won't find a bear in a cave but there is another mammal that likes to sleep in caves. Do you know what warm-blooded creature sleeps in a cave and comes out at night?

During the day bats sleep, hanging by their feet from rock ledges in cool, dark places like caves. And they don't fall off!

Bats are important in the world around us. Emerging from their cave at dusk, bats hunt and devour insects, using a form of sonar or echo-location to find their prey. Without bats we would be smothered by insects. Some bats help farmers pollinate the plants in their fields as they move from plant to plant, sucking the nectar out of the blossoms that bear fruit.

The myotis velifer or common cave bat returns each year to Karchner Caverns as the cacti and succulents begin to bloom. About 1500 adult bats raise their pups along ledges in the cave, teaching them to hunt and eco-locate. The bats follow a seasonal migration. They hunt insects through the dark night skies before returning to their roost in the cavern. Once a week, Park staff climb into the original entrance of the cave to count the bats.

If you find a bat, don't touch! They are very sensitve. If a bat is within reach, it could be injured or ill with rabies.

Bees love caves!
Caves are cool and dimly lit - a great place to build a hive. As Africanized bees have moved into Arizona, the threat of bee attack has become more frequent. If bees are flying around a cave entrance, it might be better to back off and call it a day. There are other great places waiting to be explored.

Photo used by permission of Karchner Caverns State Park

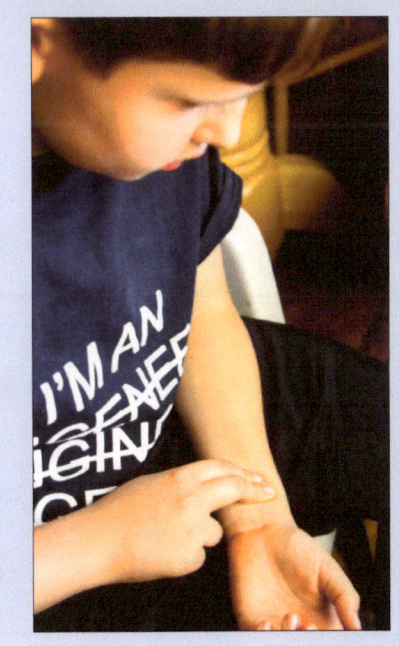

When a bat hibernates, its heart rate drops to one beat every four minutes. This allows them to hibernate for long periods of time. What would happen if your heart rate dropped this low?

Find your pulse by holding two fingers on the under-side of your wrist. Can you feel your heart beating? Count the number of beats in 15 seconds. Now multiply that number by 4. This is the number of times your heart beats in one minute.

Multiply by 4 again and this is the number of times your heart beats in four minutes. How does your heart rate compare to a bar's heart rate?

Building Blocks for a Cave

To better understand how a cave is formed we can do this simple observation. You'll need:
>modeling clay
>sugar cubes
>spray bottle with water

Begin by breaking off pieces of modeling clay and forming irregular balls as shown. Use the balls to form a circle. Fill with sugar cubes and then add more clay around the edges and top.

Don't pack the balls tightly. Just like the earth around us, the water must seep down through the balls of clay.

Once the sugar cubes have been covered with clay, use the spray bottle to spray the mound with cool water. It helps to tilt the surface under the cave slightly to allow the water to drain off. This is best done outside as the runoff will be sticky.

As the cubes melt we can remove part of the outer walls to observe the cave that has formed. Note that part of the outside has dropped to the floor of the cave just as it would with dirt and rock.

Consider where the water would runoff in a real cave. Water always seeks the low point. A cave might not be the best place when it is raining.

Some caves like Karchner Caverns have trails with lights and guides to take visitors through the cave. Others caves have been left just the way explorers found them.

What's a spelunker?

Dictionary: One who makes a hobby of exploring and studying caves.

Spelunking

Before we enter a deep, dark cave, we need to think. Think hard about what equipment we need to explore a cave. Shoes would be good. Sturdy shoes to protect our feet. Not skinny little sandals.

We know it is going to be dark. We should take a flashlight! Maybe two flashlights in case the first light quits working.

Hint: Each person should have two flashlights. A headlight works great because it leaves your hands free to grab a ledge when you stumble.

Is it warm inside a cave? Will we get cold?

Hint: Most caves are around 55 degrees fahrenheit. After being in the cave a while, that feels kind of chilly. A jacket would be good!

Serious spelunkers wear helmets because they know it hurts to hit your head on the low ceiling of a cave. And it hurts if a rock falls from the ceiling and hits you in the head.

Important! Before entering a cave, always tell someone where you are going and when you will be back. If you don't return, they should call for help!

Important: In a deep cave, always bring a guide who knows the way out! If you can't see the entrance of the cave, go back. Find an adult or a someone to help you explore the cave.

Can we learn how a cave was formed by looking at the texture and color of the rocks?

Grand Canyon Caverns

Wave Cave Photo:
Patty & Charlie Houghton

Note the red rock of Robber's Roost. This is a cave in sandstone, a porous rock. The rocks of the Lava cave appear to be volcanic while the Grand Canyon Caverns are a pale-colored rock identified as limestone. Later we'll learn more about how each type of rock is formed.

These caves are in rock. Why would a cave carved out of a hill of sand collapse? A cave hollowed out of sand is not safe to enter!

Other well known caves in Arizona

Cave of the Dome, Grand Canyon
Wind Caves, Sedona
Wave Cave, Superstition Mountains
The Cave at Cave Creek, By Tour only
Ventana Cave, Tohono O'odham Reservation
Peppersauce Cave, Santa Catalina Mountains
Cave of the Bells, Santa Rita Mountains *
Onyx Cave, Santa Rita Mountains *
Crystal Cave, Chiricahuas Mountains *
Coronado Cave, Coronado National Monument

*Kubla Khan at Karchner Caverns
Photo used by permission of Karchner Caverns State Park*

* The Cave of the Bells, Onyx Cave and Crystal Cave require a reservation with the Coronado Forest Service.

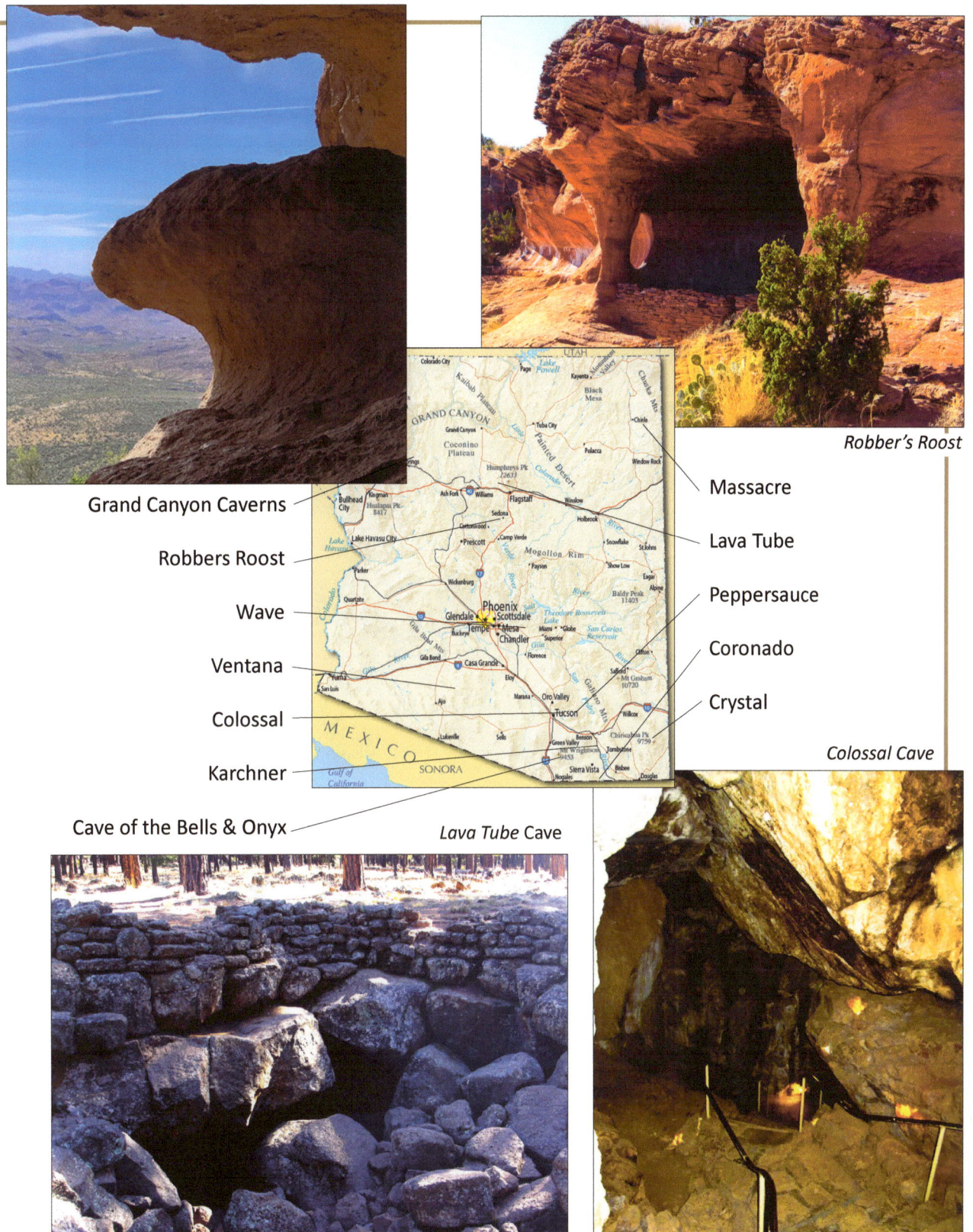

Robber's Roost

Colossal Cave

Lava Tube Cave

- Grand Canyon Caverns
- Robbers Roost
- Wave
- Ventana
- Colossal
- Karchner
- Cave of the Bells & Onyx
- Massacre
- Lava Tube
- Peppersauce
- Coronado
- Crystal

Can you imagine a hill upside-down?

If you're like me, your imagination can't quite see a hill that is upside down.

Sinkholes are formed when an underground cavern collapses due to the weight of the earth above it. Often the cavern is formed by water. Imagine a stream that is hidden underground. The stream slowly begins to carry the dirt away and a cave begins to form. When the cave can no longer support the weight of the ceiling, gravity pulls the ceiling down with dirt and rock falling to the floor below. This is a sinkhole.

Two well known sinkholes are located in Sedona, the Devil's Kitchen and the Devil's Dining Room. Both remain somewhat active so we don't play around the edges of sinkholes. Notice the big rocks

Sink holes

Devil's Kitchen Sinkhole

that have caved off the edge of the Devil's Kitchen.

In the White Mountains, the Canyon Point Sinkhole happened many years ago. After the ground settled, grasses and trees began to take root in the loose soil. As water flowed into the sinkhole from the rim, the trees grew very tall. One tree was so big, four people could barely encircle the trunk holding hands. In time, the big trees were attacked by bark beetles and began to die. Now, little trees have begun to grow, replacing what was lost.

The Canyon Point Sinkhole has been stable for years and people walk down into the sinkhole regularly. It is very quiet down in the pit as if the noise has been left on the rim.

Devil's Kitchen & Devil's Diningroom

Canyon Point Sink hole

Not all big holes in the ground are caves. In 1877, a man named David Gowan was searching the canyons of the Tonto Basin for gold when he first discovered a natural bridge. The local tribes often camped along the creek near the bridge, raising crops during warm weather. Like his neighbors, David planted a garden with an orchard. The Apaches did not always want David living there as their neighbor. During one conflict, David hid for three days in the cave under the bridge until the threat had passed.

The bridge is 183 feet high, the tunnel under the bridge is 393 feet long. Pine Creek flows through five pools under the bridge.

Welcome to Tonto Natural Bridge!

Bridges & Arches

"Gavin, look! Cool, delicious, clear water. Look closely! Do you see anything in the water?"

"Maybe I see a bug."

"I wasn't thinking about bugs, Gavin. This water may look clear but it carries tiny grains of carbonite minerals. As the water flows down the hillside, the minerals form layers of rock called travertine. This bridge is travertine rock."

"So, you're telling me the water carries a mineral that we can't see? If I drink this water, will those minerals start to grow inside me?"

"I don't think you have to worry about a bridge bursting out of your stomach one day. Your body gets rid of the minerals you don't need to grow."

"So building this bridge one grain at a time must have taken a long time."

"Scientists have measured the deposits in the water below and say travertine forms at about an inch and a half each year."

"That's really cool, dad. Where does the water come from to build the bridge?"

"Pine Creek is fed by springs in the mountains above this canyon. Snowmelt and rain also send water into the stream. If we look closely we will find a small spring on the hillside below the visitor's center. The water in the spring has been stored underground for thousands of years and once flowed out onto the hillside."

"I'm ready to jump into some cool water!"

"Gavin! Be careful!"

"Owww!"

"Gavin, are you all right?"

"Oww! That really hurt!"

"You can't just race into the water. These rocks are really slick! The water makes algae grow on the rocks and when we step on it, our feet slide out from under us and we land on the rocks. You can be seriously hurt! Gavin, are you sure you're OK?"

"Yeah, Dad. I think I'm OK. Nothing seems to be broken but let's sit here for a moment. Are there more bridges like this in Arizona?"

To see the effect of ice on rock, drop an ice cube into a glass of water at room temperature.

Did the ice crack? Pull the ice out of the water and examine the fractures. Are the cracks along straight lines or did the cracks wander through the cube of ice?

What does this tell us about the water seeping into the cracks of rock cliffs when it freezes as the temperatures drop? Would the freezing water force the cracks wider and break the rock? What whould happen if you were standing under the rock when it breaks?

Do you know the difference between a bridge and an arch?

Let's start with what a natural bridge and an arch have in common. Both are carved from rock by natural forces like wind, water or ice. Both have a narrow span of rock with an empty center. Both an arch and a bridge are linked to the earth at both ends.

An arch may be carved away from a rock cliff while a bridge always spans a gap between two landing points. The big difference seems to be that water or at least a creek bed flows under a bridge. An arch may or may not have water under it but an arch is generally not used as a bridge.

White Mesa Arch

Confused?

This is a picture of a bridge though it is called Vultee Arch. Maybe the person who named the arch didn't know the difference.

Before an arch is created, a wall of rock stood tall. The wind began to pick at tiny cracks in the rock. Rain and melted snow flowed down the surface of the rock, freezing and widening the cracks in the cliff. The wind picked at a tiny hole in the rock. Through seasons of freezing and thawing, small chunks of rock fell, enlarging the hole. Over the years, the hole grew until one day a kid just like you looked up at the natural rock arch and wondered how that hole was created.

An arch or bridge reminds us that something far more powerful than our mortal muscles is at work in the world around us. These natural formations have left people in awe for years and inspired men and women to create great architecture.

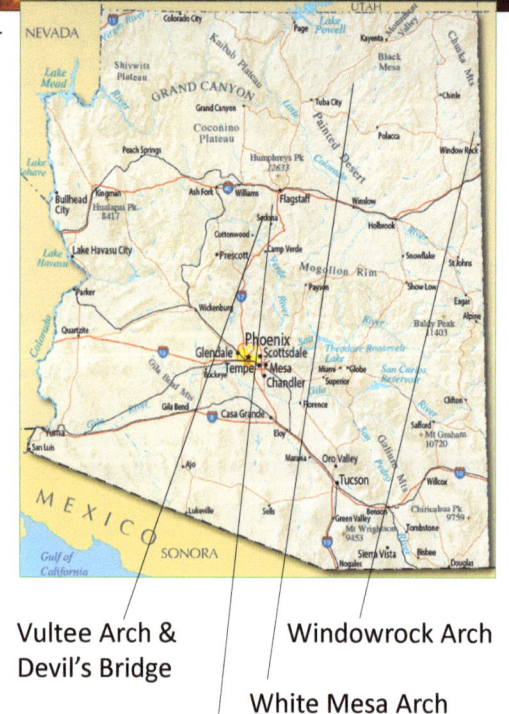

Rainbow Bridge is one of the iconic symbols of our state, recognized all over the world. The bridge is actually located in Utah but accessed from Arizona, either by a long hike or by boat. Photo: David F. Menne

Angels Window

Vultee Arch & Devil's Bridge

Windowrock Arch

White Mesa Arch

Slide Rock Arch

Windowrock Arch is sacred to the Navajos. The tribe requests that visitors not climb to the arch.

White Mesa Arch seen as a window, the other side as an arch.

There are over 100 arches, bridges and windows identified in Arizona. For a good reference check out Bob's Arches - Arizona online. These are just seven of the better known formations in Arizona.

Vultee Arch

Devil's Bridge

Slide Rock Arch

The Mines
A Big Hole in the Ground

"Gavin, you know I gave your mom a special ring when we got married. Do you know what metal is in that ring?"

"Is it gold?"

"Yes, do you know where the gold came from?"

"We talked about mining for gold in school."

"A mine is a deep hole in the ground that follows a streak of ore. Sometimes the hole looks like a tunnel. Other mines are big pits, open to the sky."

"Gavin, let me tell you about two mines in Arizona. The Lavender Pit in Bisbee was once the biggest open pit copper mine in the United States. Ledges along the walls of the pit allowed big trucks to carry the ore up to the top. The trucks had tires that were taller than me!"

"Tires over six feet tall?"

"That's right. Today, some of the tires on mining trucks are closer to 10 feet high.

The drivers need a ladder to climb into their trucks."

"Wow! You could run over anything with a truck that big!"

"When they were digging the Lavender Pit, they had to move some of the houses so they would not fall into the big hole."

"You mean people had to move just because they were digging up the ground for a mine?"

"That's right, Gavin. One day, the company that owned the mine decided they couldn't find enough ore to keep on mining so they closed the mine."

"Is the hole is still there."

"That's right! We can stand on the edge and see where the big trucks once carried the ore."

"What about tunnel mines, Dad?"

"In the early days of Arizona, men and

Photo: Mining truck P. Payette

Lavender Pit

women dug tunnels into the mountains to find gold and silver. We find these old tunnels all over Arizona, some still active. Your grandpa worked in one of the underground mines. Thousands of men worked underground so that we would have the metal we need for the items we used everyday."

"How did they dig out the rock, Dad?"

"They used long metal bits to drill into the rock. In these deep holes the men planted explosives and blasting caps that would explode after they left the area. The explosives broke up the rock. When the men returned, they would load the ore onto carts pulled by a train out of the mine."

"Dad, could we visit an underground mine?"

"Gavin, if we're going into a mine, we're going to need some special clothing to protect us. Then, a little train will take us through a tunnel to where the men used to dig the ore. Can you imagine working underground with the all that dirt and rock above your head?"

"Whoa! I'm not sure I would like that."

"You asked for a tour. If we go to the town of Bisbee in southern Arizona, we can see the Lavender Pit and take a tour of an underground mine. The men who give the tours worked underground years ago. They can tell us how the work was done."

"Dad, that's sounds awesome. Let's take a tour of the mine!"

Gavin stands at the entrance of the Copper Queen mine.

The copper mining industry played a big part in helping our state grow. Along with copper, miners dug up turquoise that is made into beautiful

Are you up to a stair climb?
Mining towns have a lot of stairs as they are often built on a hillside. Bisbee, the home of the Copper Queen mine, has an annual event called the Bisbee 1000. Runners climb up and down lots of stairs over four and a half miles!

Gavin's Tip

Arizona has old mines all over the state. Sometimes the entrance is open to the sky and it is easy to stumble into the mine. Some people have tried to explore the old mines and had an accident. Falling into a mine is more adventure than I want to find! If you find an old mine, don't enter it. Just remember the miners who helped Arizona grow into a state.

Panning for Gold

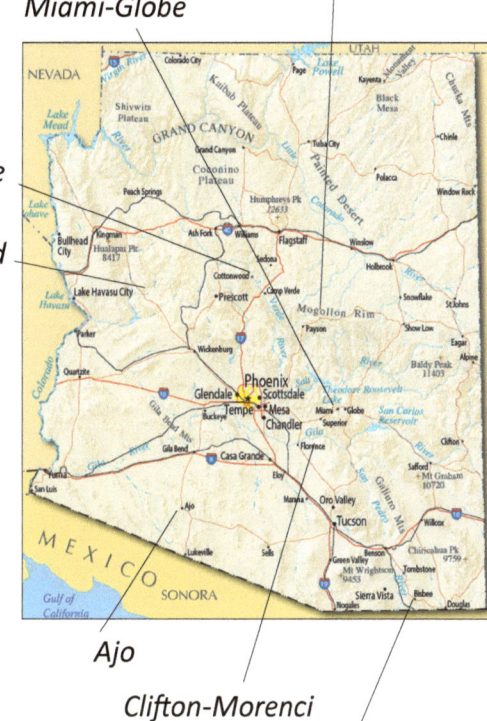

Railroad Tunnel
Miami-Globe
Jerome
Bagdad
Ajo
Clifton-Morenci
Bisbee & the Copper Queen tour

Like the old propectors, people wander the mountains of Arizona, panning for gold just like Gavin is watching in this demonstration.

29

A Man-made Tunnel

We've looked at arches, bridges and caves but one cave was not made by wind or water. This cave is a tunnel that was created for the mining industry.

The tunnel, conceived by an ambitious man, is located on a steep hillside overlooking the Tonto Basin.

James Eddy wanted to ship rock ore from the mines in Globe up to Flagstaff where the rocks would be loaded onto trains. Once shipped to the smelter, the valuable minerals could be removed from the rock. As part of the route for his railroad he dreamed of building a tunnel 3,100 feet in length through the cliffs of the Mogollon Rim. In August 1883, his men began digging the tunnel but James Eddy soon ran out of money. He never did finish the tunnel. If the tunnel had been completed, the old steam locomotives would have had difficulty climbing the steep grade.

The historic Arizona Mineral Belt Railroad tunnel.

Today, 70 feet of the original tunnel remains open. The tunnel is visited by people of all ages. If we are very quiet near the cave, we may find other visitors too. Sometimes, the deer and elk quietly approach the entrance to get a drink from water than collects on the tunnel floor.

"Gavin, do you know what a volcano is?"

"Sure, volcanoes are mountains that spit fire, Dad. They erupt, spewing ash and lava. I learned about volcanoes in school."

"Look down at your feet. Can you imagine hot rock and fire under the soles of your shoes?"

"This looks like grass to me, Dad."

"Trust me! Deep under the surface of the earth the rocks are very hot. So hot the rocks flow like the syrup over your pancakes."

Standing on Hot Ground

Volcanoes

Looking at Humphries Peak

"When a volcano becomes active, fire, gas and rock erupt through the surface of the earth."

"Does Arizona have any volcanoes, Dad?"

"You're climbing one right now, Gavin!"

"Whoa! This is a volcano? Are we safe?"

"Gavin, this volcano has been silent for a long time. It hasn't erupted in centuries. Let me show you a rock. Does it tell you a story?"

"Dad, there isn't any story in this rock."

"Gavin, when I look at this rock, I'm trying to breathe but it is really smoky with ash in the air. There are rocks on fire falling around me. The earth is shaking."

"Dad, none of that is in this old rock. Are you feeling OK?"

"Look again, Gavin. What color is the rock?"

"Black."

"Black like a cinder. Burned black like this rock was once on fire. If you feel

the surface you might guess that this rock is very brittle. Hit the rock with a piece of iron and it might shatter into pieces. This rock is called obsidian and the native Americans used the flakes from this rock as arrowheads. The edges are very sharp, like glass."

"Dad, could this volcano become active again?"

"The lava that once flowed from this mountain has receded and we can say the mountain has gone to sleep for centuries. I don't think we have much to worry about but just over a thousand years ago, the people living here had to move away from Sunset Crater. The cinder cone was belching smoke and ashes. Rock bombs were falling and fiery streams of lava were creeping close to their homes."

"Wow, that must have been kind of scary."

"Gavin, let's visit the remains of an old lava flow at Sunset Crater. Using your imagination, you might be able to see the lava on fire as it moved into the forest."

The San Francisco Peaks are an ancient stratovolcano. Today six peaks line the edges of the crater. All six are over 11,000 feet high. The crater is called the inner basin and is a popular place for recreation.

Humphreys, 12,643 feet
Agassiz Peak, 12,356 feet
Fremont Peak, 11,969 feet
Aubineau Peak, 11,838 feet
Rees Peak, 11,474 feet
Doyle Peak, 11,460 feet

The Humphrey's Peak trail takes hikers from the Arizona Snow Bowl four and a half miles to the summit of Mount Humphrey, with views that stretch to the Grand Canyon and the Verde Valley.

Arizona was once a hot spot for volcanos. The two tallest mountains in our state are dormant volcanoes. Arizona has over 600 dormant cinder cones. To say a volcano is dormant means they have not erupted in hundreds of years.

The tallest mountain in our state, Mount Humphreys, was once part of a much taller mountain that stood high over the forests of Arizona. Many centuries ago, the lava began to move upward inside the mountain until the peak could no longer withstand the pressure. The molten rock, gas and ash burst outward from the mountain. During the eruption, the mountain lost so much rock and dirt that the peak collapsed, forming a crater called a caldera. We could say the mountain blew it's top!

Rock, ash and hot gas flew into the air. Huge rocks, called lava bombs, exploded as they fell to earth. Lava flows crept down the side of the peak, through the forest below. We can still see the remains of these lava flows in the forest north of Flagstaff. As the dust and ash settled, the lava began to cool into hard black ridges. Today we can climb up the side of the San Francisco Peaks and peer down into the crater. We won't find any lava or fire. Instead tall pines, aspen and fir trees cover the slopes of the volcano. Thick grass has covered areas that don't have trees, making the crater a nice place for a picnic on a warm day.

Before this volcano erupted it was one peak, Now, six peaks line the rim of the crater. This volcano is a classic stratovolcano with steep sides surrounding a central vent.

The San Francisco Peaks are located in a bed of cinder cones. Mount Elden, the ridge southeast of the Peaks, is a shield volcano. As it erupted, the lava formed a plate around the vent, building up layer after layer instead of the classic cone.

On the eastern side of our state, near Springerville, is another cluster of cinder cones. Turkey Creek Caldera is located in the southeastern part of our state. You might say that Arizona was a hot bed of volcanic activity.

Today, lots of people like to hike the trail to the top of Mount Humphreys during the summer months. In the winter, the top is covered by snow and only a few make it to the top of the mountain. They take special equipment to get through the deep snow. Others prefer to ride a chair lift up the mountain and ski down over the snowy slopes.

When the cold winter wind creeps inside our coats, we tend to forget that this was once a very hot, smoky place.

Gavin: "After climbing the Bonita lava flow, I could see how far the black rock had spread from the Sunset Crater. This is not a good place to slip and fall!"

'Malpais'

When the Spanish came to the North American continent, they discovered black, coarse rock piled in waves spreading across vast areas like this lava flow. Their horses and cattle could not walk across the rough surface. The Spanish called the region 'malpais,' meaning bad land. This is a lava flow that has cooled and hardened. Notice there are no green plants growing in the waves of rock one thousand years after the volcano spit out the lava to cover the forest floor.

Malpais has a pitted surface, showing that gas bubbles in the rock burst as the rock cooled. Can you imagine what it would have been like to stand here and watch the lava rush toward you?

Why did ancient Native Americans used obsidian for arrowheads?

When chipped, the edges of obsidian are very narrow and sharp. They cut like a piece of broken glass. Native Americans used obsidian for arrow points and quartz rock for spear points. When exploring the sites where these ancient people once lived, we may find old arrowheads laying on the ground.

Native Americans used bone or stone hammers to chip and shape a promising chunk of quartz or obsidian. Then, using the base of a deer antler, they chipped fragments from the rock to form the shape of an arrow or spear point.

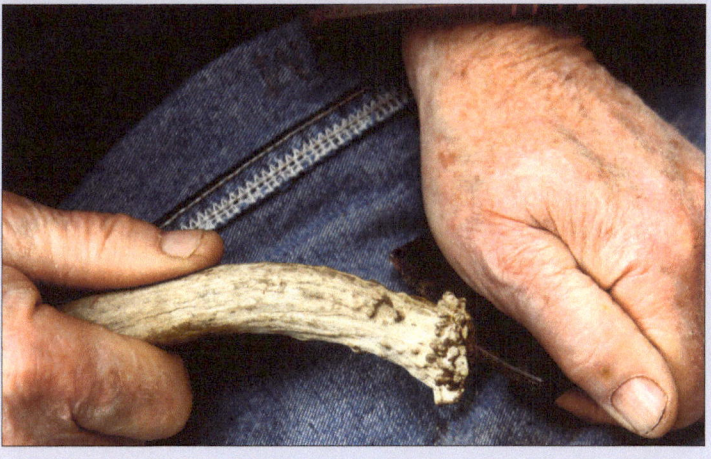

If making an arrowhead, the craftsman would use the tip of the antler to chip small fragments from the edge of an obsidian arrowhead, creating a razor-sharp edge.

To fasten the arrowhead to the shaft of the arrow, the craftsman would notch the blunt end of the stone point as shown on the arrowhead above. Then he would bind the arrow point to the shaft with deer sinew or cactus twine.

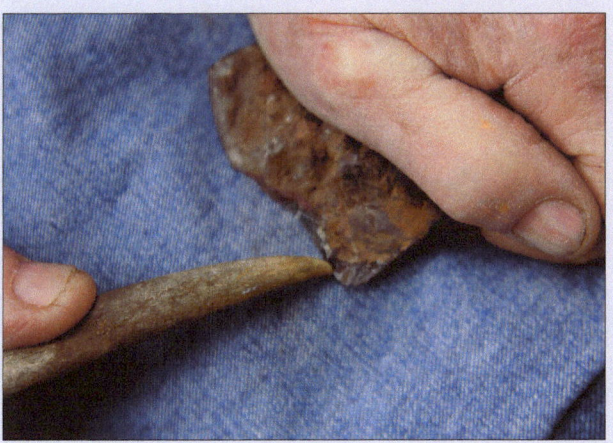

This is Sunset Crater. Can you see that the cinders on the peak are red while the cinders at the base are black. What caused the cinders to be different colors?

* Temperature?

* Mineral composition?

* Paint?

Most likely the cinders differ in color based on the quantity of iron present in the rock.

After Sunset Crater stopped erupting and grew quiet, the people returned to the plain surrounding the volcano. Digging through the ash, they found that the cinders helped retain moisture and contained minerals that grew good crops.

They built their homes along the rim of silent cinder cones where a little heat from deep beneath the earth lingered within the craters. We can still see the remains of these primitive homes in the caves atop Old Caves Crater. Across Arizona, we see the shallow pits used by those who lived in pit houses long ago.

The site of an ancient pit house at the summit of old Caves Crater, outside Flagstaff.

Lava River Cave

"Dad, there's a big hole in the ground!"

"What do you see around the hole, Gavin?"

"There seems to be a lot of rock but I think I see a way inside. Can we climb down and see what is in there?"

"Maybe a bear?"

"Really, dad? We already talked about a bear."

"Gavin, I'm teasing you. This is the work of a volcano. We think of lava as being a pile of jumbled rock. Sometimes, the outside of a lava flow begins to cool as the rocks inside remains fiery hot. What do you think happens then, Gavin?"

"Can the inside keep moving? Does it pull the rocks on the outside along with it?"

"No, the outside stays right where it began to cool while the inside of the lava flow keeps moving. As the inner core moves forward, a tunnel or cave is created. That's what made this big hole in the ground. Watch your step, Gavin!"

"Dad, I think we need a flashlight! This is really dark!"

"I just happen to have a flashlight for you and a flashlight for me! Did you bring your jacket?"

"I didn't think I would need a jacket since it is kind of hot outside."

"One thing about a cave, the temperature remains fairly constant with all this rock around it. You're going to find that the temperature in this cave is cool. Look over here for a minute."

"Is that ice?"

"You're right! During the winter, water seeps around the entrance of the cave and then freezes when night comes. The ice often remains long after the outside temperatures begin to warm."

"Dad, I'm not hot anymore and this rock under our feet is really rough."

"Well, Gavin, we are walking on a lava flow. Hang onto that flashlight. If you drop

Huge boulders jumble down along the entrance of the Lava cave making the climb inside challenging.

it, the light might slide into a crack and we won't find it again."

"How long is this tunnel?"

"The tunnel goes back about three quarters of a mile. Look to the side here. Do you see another passage?"

"Where does that go?"

"You see how the ceiling of the tunnel ahead seems to drop? If we kept going, we would have to crawl through a low spot. This side tunnel goes around to the end of the tunnel where the ceiling isn't so low. Which way are we going to go, Gavin?"

"I want to see both sides. Let's do this one first."

"We'll take a moment to stop and sit. Now turn off your flashlight."

"Dad, this is really dark. I can hear myself breathe!"

"That's right, Gavin. We understand how dark it can get when we walk through a lava tunnel. Unlike the dark skies at night, there isn't even a trace of starlight."

"I'm glad I have a flashlight!"

"Gavin, there is another kind of rock that comes from a volcano. Do you remember when I talked about how smoky the skies could be during an eruption?"

"You said it would be hard to breathe."

"That's right. When a large volcano explodes, it blows steam and ash with chunks of rock into the sky. As gravity pulls the ash back to earth, the ash forms a layer of tuff. As the tuff hardens, it is called rhyolite tuff. A good place to find rhyolite tuff is in the Chiricahua Mountains."

"So what this rock look like?"

"Like rock!"

"You're funny, Dad. What's makes it so special?"

"As water and ice begin to seep into the cracks, the rock is eroded into pillars of stone called hoodoos."

"Hoodoos?"

"The Apaches called the Chiricahuas in southern Arizona the 'land of the standing

Making a miniature caldera

Don't pack the sand down.

You are going to need:
a bucket of sand and a balloon

Take a deep breath! Blow up the ballon to about 8 inches in diameter and tie a knot so the air does not escape.

Next place the balloon in a container like a bucket or box. Cover the balloon with sand. Don't pack it down. Next, use something sharp to pop the balloon, causing the sand to sink rapidly in the middle. Go ahead, shove something sharp into the balloon.

What happened?

Did the sand remain level or did all the sand collapse with the balloon? If you bump the bucket, does the sand along the sides collapse like a landslide?

We found that a slight crater formed with the outer edges higher than the center. If we had used a smaller balloon, our crater might have retained steeper walls.

Lava may move toward the earth's surface very fast and burst out in a cloud of steam and ash called a pyroclastic cloud moving at 400 to 500 miles an hour. A volcano with a pyroclastic explosion may lose so much rock and soil that the interior collapses leaving a crater behind. Only the largest craters, like that of the San Francisco Peaks are called calderas.

Cinder Cones

Calderas

Sand dunes

40

up rock.' Some hoodoos are pillars of rocks. Others look like giant stones balanced on a tiny base."

"This looks like a great place for a game of hide and seek."

"The Apaches hid among these rocks as they fought against the arrival of white people into a land they considered their home. This section of the Chiricahuas is a National Park called the Wonderland of Rocks."

"I like what the Apaches called it better. *The Land of the Standing Up Rocks*!"

"As we walk through the Park, we'll see huge rocks balanced on little pedestals and giant columns towering over us."

"So what volcano blew out the ash to make these columns?"

"We're standing near the Turkey Creek Caldera which erupted long before people came to live here."

"This is so different from the malpais lava flow at Sunset Crater."

"Gavin, we've seen four features of volcanoes all within Arizona. Do you remember them all?"

* The San Francisco Peaks, a dormant volcano.
* The Bonito Lava Flow below Sunset Crater.
* The Lava River Cave
* The hoodoos of the Chiricahua Mountains.

"Sounds like an adventure to me, dad."

Are all mountains made by volcanoes?

NO

LIMESTONE

Lava is volcanic rock deposited on the earth's surface but some rocks are formed one grain at a time.

Limestone is a deposit made from the accumulation of shell, coral, algae and skeletons of dead sea creatures combined with calcium carbonate in shallow water. Though we think of Arizona as a desert region, ancient lakes once covered part of our state.

Limestone is a light-colored rock. When we look at a cliff that is light colored we have to ask, 'Is that made from ground shells or from sand?'

Above: Sand Dunes along I-8
Opposite page: Sandstone Cliff - Oak Creek

Sandstone

Wind and rain, helped by freezing temperatures, break rocks into tiny grains we call sand.

Some visitors think our state is covered by sand. They are surprised to find pine-covered peaks trees and big lakes in Arizona! As the rocks break down, much of the sand washes down from the mountains to create big basins of sand and grit in the southern part of the state.

Imagine sliding down a sand dune on a sled? Or roaring over the top in a dune buggy. Sand is not just for the beach!

Arizona sand dunes are a favorite playground for kids of all ages with four-wheel-drive machines. They roar across the dunes, the sand swirling upward in their wake. Keep moving! Don't let your tires dig into the sand and get stuck!

Did you know sand naturally comes in at least 4 colors? Green, Red, White and Brown.

"Gavin, do you remember the black rock I gave you when we were talking about volcanoes?"

"Obsidian? It was hard, black and shiny."

"Here's another rock for you. Tell me what story this rock gives you."

"This rock is gritty. It feels like I'm rubbing sand off the surface."

"Gavin, when I touch this rock, I see

Walls of Sand

a shallow sea stretching out in front of us. Little bits of sand are filtering down through the water. Big sand dunes are forming, all under water. Take a look around us. Do you see the sand dunes?"

"No, I don't see dunes. I see rock cliffs. Could the cliffs have been sand at one time, dad?"

"Good guess, Gavin. Think about the shallow sea and grains of sand drifting down through the water? Over the years, all those grains built big ridges of sand. Under the pressure of the water, the sand hardened into rock."

"How did the rock rise out of the water, dad?"

"Our earth is constantly shifting. These cliffs were pushed upward by pressure from beneath the surface. The water covering the rocks drained into lower areas. Run your hand over this rock. What do you feel?"

"I feel a dip that runs across the rock."

"You're right. Each time it rains hard the water drains off the rocks, along this channel.

"If you look around, you can see how the water has shaped the surface of these cliffs."

"You're telling me that the water is carving the rocks?"

"Not just water. Ice and wind also do their part to shape the rock."

Water

"Dad, look at that cliff over there. Do you see the dark streaks coming down the face of the cliff?"

"You have good eyes! Water flows down the face of the cliff, it leaves a dark stain. Gavin, do you think water is important in Arizona?"

"Dad, we live in a desert! Of course, water is important!"

"OK, we both think water is important. But how and why is water important?"

"I see a lot more trees and grass near water. The desert doesn't have a lot of trees and there isn't much water there either."

"Gavin, we looked at volcanoes from four different points of view. I think we should look at water in different ways. We might first ask where water comes from?"

"That's easy! Water comes from the sky as rain or snow."

"We do get rain and snow in Arizona but some water comes to us from underground. What if I showed you a place where water flows out of rock? Think of water bubbling up from a hole to cover your feet, then your knees. As you walk through the stream, the water comes up to your waist. All of that water is coming from a hole in the ground."

Snow in the Desert

We think of the desert as HOT. We know snow is cold. Can it snow in the desert?

Water comes in three forms: liquid, solid and gas. If the desert is hot, we would think that it could not snow in the desert but it does! During the winter, when the temperature drops to 32 degrees Fahrenheit, water begins to freeze, changing from a liquid into a solid form. If we want to see snow on our cactus, the temperature must drop to 32 degrees or colder when it is raining. Yes, it does snow in the desert in Arizona!

The next time it rains, run outside with an indoor-outdoor thermometer and check the temperature to see if there is any chance of snow. While you're out there, splash in the puddles, do a rain dance and celebrate good water!

"That sounds awesome. Is there such a place in Arizona?"

"You bet! I'm describing a spring. In many places, water is trapped under the ground, sometimes in little cracks, in other places as pools of water. This is called an aquifer. A spring appears when water trapped underground finds a crack

"Hey, you took me there last year. There was a lot of water in that stream, Dad."

"If we walked upstream from the pools we swam in, we would find the springs bubbling out of the ground. One flows from the creek bank, another spring bubbles up in the middle of the streambed. Just think how much water is trapped underground so that a

Wet Stuff

in a rock layer and begins to seep into the open air. Springs may leak onto the ground or flow out in a stream. Some springs dry up for a few months, others just keep flowing year after year. One of my favorite places is Fossil Creek down in the Verde Valley."

stream could flow day and night, year after year."

"Year after year?"

"More years than you have been alive."

"Wow, dad! That's a lot of water. Can we drink the water and swim in the pools?"

"Sometimes the water is safe to drink.

How do we know if water is safe to drink?

This water looks delicious, clean and clear. Is it safe? No! It could be swimming with bacteria from a source upstream. When drinking natural water outdoors, use a water filter to clear out the bacteria that would make you sick.

"Gavin! Take a look! How many pools do you see along the ledge?"

"One, two, uh, I think I count seven."

"How did these holes get here?"

"Did the water drain off the mountain along this ledge?"

"You're thinking! Water crept into cracks along this ledge and dissolved the rock over many years creating each of these pools. Let's see which is the deepest one. Pull out your measuring tape."

"I guess the deepest one is at the bottom, Dad. Do they keep the water all year round?"

"Yes, all year round. Native people used tinajas like these pools as a source of water."

"I don't think I would want to drink this water. It looks kind of dirty. "

"I guess that depends on just how thirsty you are. I'm sure the wildlife in this area use the pools."

'Tinaja' is the Spanish word for an earthen jar but it could also mean a pool of water in a hollow in the rock.

Before drinking from a stream, we should check whether it has been contaminated by people or animals. Some springs have been channeled into a pipe which helps protect the water source. Water with a lot of minerals, like sulfur, will smell bad."

"Dad, good drinking water is important but I also love playing in the water. Are there other waterfalls besides Fossil Creek in Arizona?"

"We have some awesome

Bubbling up . . . Splashing over . . . Big, big GULP

waterfalls. Most people think Arizona is a dry, arid region and they would be mostly right. When we do get rain or snow, the water sinks into the ground. If there is too much water for the soil to absorb, it has to go someplace. The water flows into our rivers and streams. Waterfalls show up when a stream drops over a cliff or hillside."

"Dad, have you ever swam behind a waterfall?"

"Yes, I swam to a cave behind a waterfall. We can't swim behind every waterfall as the current may be too strong."

Where the Aquifers Live

We can think of an aquifer as a place to store water underground. For this observation you will need:
   2 plastic cups
   2 straws
   gravel and sand

Poke a small hole in the bottom edge of each cup as shown in the picture - a hole that is just a little smaller than the straw.

Push the straw into the hole about one inch. Place each cup on a plate. With the straw in place, fill one cup with gravel, the other cup with sand. Slowly pour a cup of water into each cup. Don't allow the water to overflow the cup.

How much water flows from each cup? Is more water coming from one than the other? Which cup holds the water the longest?

You have created an aquifer like we might find underground. Which do you think stores more water?

1. An aquifer with big rocks?
2. An aquifer filled with gravel and sand?

Three of Arizona's best known waterfalls are found in Havasupai Canyon. People come from all over the world just to visit those falls. Havasupai, Mooney and Beaver Falls create beautiful blue-green pools with travertine deposits where visitors soak in the mineral-laced waters surrounded by soaring cliffs and green trees.

Sycamore Falls

Workman Creek Falls

We cannot drive to the land of the blue-green water as the falls are located in a deep canyon. Visitors must walk, ride a mule or a helicopter to the village of Supai. The falls are located two miles below the village of Supai.

Let's consider a few other falls that are well known in Arizona. Most flow only a few months out of the year.

Every spring, runoff from the eastern mountains fills the Little Colorado River, crashing over Grand Falls. The brown current reminds some children of chocolate milk though Gavin would not like the sticks and the trash floating in the current.

Fossil Creek is a fee area. Visitors are required to use a permit system.

That's me! Riding the Falls.

Parents, we don't recommend this. Always check the force of the current, the depth and power of the falls before allowing a child to jump with a waterfall!

What does one cubic foot of water look like?

Scientists measure the flow of water in cubic feet per minute or per second.

Imagine holding a basketball. The ball would be similar in size to one cubic foot. Now, imagine thousands of basket balls cascading over a waterfall. That would be a lot of basketballs. It would be too difficult for us to measure the flow of a waterfall like Fossil Creek. We could measure the flow on a small spring and learn how scientist measure the flow of water.

You'll need about a 12" x 12" sheet of metal or plastic, 1/8" thick, with a v- cut at the top. Build a rock dam on a small stream, inserting the plate into a gap.

As water starts to rise and flow through the 'V', grab a one-gallon milk container and place the container against the gap, allowing container to fill. Use a watch with a second hand to time how long it takes to fill the bucket. Make a note of the time.

Empty the container and repeat this process 9 more times. Record the time for each refill. When finished, add the numbers together and divided by 10.

The result tells us how fast the current in the stream is flowing or how many cubic feet of water is passing down the streambed in one minute. Can you imagine how fast it would be flowing to knock you over when standing in the middle of the stream?

The water from the stream is funneled through the v-shape gap.

West of Flagstaff, water from a wildlife tank drops over rocky cliffs to fill a sunken meadow called Keyhole Sink. Children like Gavin love playing in the water and finding the petroglyphs scattered on the cliffs around the sink.

South of Keyhole Sink and hidden in a steep canyon is Sycamore Falls. This waterfall is in a popular rock-climbing area called Paradise Forks. There is a route to climb down into the canyon but those viewing the falls from the top should take extra care that the edge of the rim does not drop out from under their feet.

Workman Creek drops into another of the state's long falls. The creek is in the Sierra Anchas, east of Roosevelt Lake, and has become a popular spot for those who like exploring the back country of our state.

Cibeque Creek is reached by swimming or wading up the stream to the falls in a small canyon that drains into the Salt River. The same is true of Ellison Creek where it falls into the East Verde River, north of Payson. A flood recently raged through Ellison Creek as a tragic flash flood, catching visitors unaware.

Mooney Falls on Cataract Creek, Havasupai. The trail to bottom of the falls descends a cliff, passing through a cave and down a ladder. The rocks around the falls are travertine just like at Tonto Natural Bridge. Here the rock's contour mimics the falls.

In a narrow canyon, it is always wise to be aware of the weather upstream and whether rain might flood the narrow canyons.

For those who living in southern Arizona, the Seven Falls telescoping down the cliffs of Bear Canyon are a favorite swimming area each spring.

These are just a few of Arizona's better known waterfalls.

Seven Falls

We live in a desert. Even our mountains don't have a lot of water. Can you imagine running out of water?
Nothing to drink! No water to wash!
How can we conserve water for the future?

**Here are some ways
you can help save water:**

- Turn off the water when you're not actively using it, like when brushing your teeth.
- Take fast showers - don't stand there for 20 minutes.
- Use dirty water or water left from meals and chores to water plants.
- Skip washing the car and the dog. Sweep sidewalks and driveway instead of using the hose.
- Tell your parents when a faucett is leaking so they can fix it.

Gavin's Hint:
I'll skip a bath tonight!

Gavin's Mom:
NO!

Grand Falls, Sometimes called Chocolate Falls

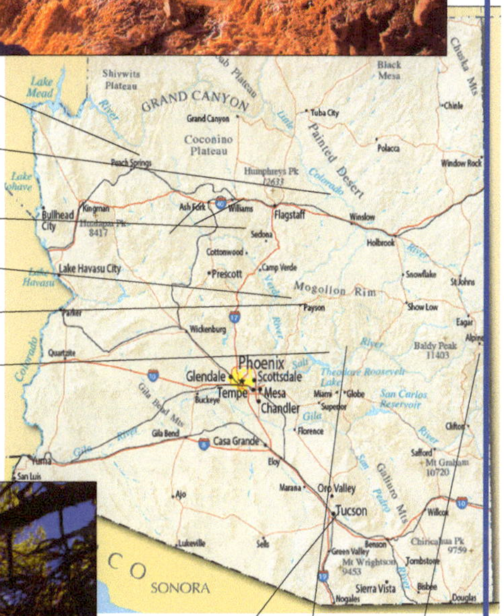

Havasupai & Mooney Falls

Grand Falls of the Little Colorado River *

Sycamore & Keyhole Sink Falls *

Fossil Creek Wilderness

Ellison Creek Falls

Workman Creek Falls *

* Seasonal

Seven Falls *

Cibeque Falls - requires permit

KP Creek Falls

Keyhole Sink

"Dad, with all this talk about waterfalls and cool water I want to go swimming. Are there other good places to go swimming in Arizona?"

"Your swimming pool, Gavin."

"Funny, dad. I mean places with real water like creeks and swimming holes."

"I know what you mean, Gavin. We could call streams *natural water*. Do you know the difference between a natural lake and a reservoir held behind a dam?"

"I know what a dam is since we visited the dam up at Lake Powell."

"A natural lake is like a bowl as shown in the clay model below. Water drains into the bowl and forms a lake. Sometimes a stream flows into a lake and out the other end. A reservoir is created when a dam is built across a stream and water collects behinded the dam. Remember last year when our family went to Lake Pleasant. You rode the wake board with your big brother?"

"Oh, that was so much fun!"

"Lake Pleasant is a reservoir. Without the dam, the lake would not be there."

"I guess dams can be a good thing in our desert, dad."

"We're saving the water behind our dams for the years when we don't have much water coming down in rain or snow. We can play in those lakes, too, when our temperatures get really hot. Do you want to visit Lake Pleasant this summer?

"Yes! I want to go again. This time I'll ride my own board!"

I was just a little guy in this picture!

Clay model of a lake

and a reservoir.

Doing the Creek

I'm going to . . .

swim

tickle a fish

catch a crawdad

(I will not let the crawdad catch me)

collect shiny rocks

race leaf boats

look for frogs

splash my sister / brother

build a dam

skip a rock

explore under water with goggles

catch a water strider

   or maybe some pollywogs

Wake board surfing with my big brother!

This pool is fed by a small hot spring along the Colorado River.

Hot Springs

Think back to what we learned about volcanoes. The lava in our volcanoes has receded deep underground but the heat from the lava still warms some of our aquifers. When a warm aquifer emerges, we call it a hot spring. You know what a hot tub is; warm springs are nature's hot tubs. Check out the map for some of Arizona's hot springs. They are listed in red on the next page.

Gavin's Tip: Check the temperature of a hot spring before you jump in.

More than 20 favorite swimming holes.

**Hot springs have been designated in red.
We have not listed all of the hot springs as some are located on private land.
Check with the Forest Service or governing office before visiting an area for any restrictions.**

- Ringbolt HS & Arizona HS
- Virgin River CGs
- Havasupai
- Lake Powell
- Wheatfields Lake
- Colorado River - Willow Beach
- Clear Creek Reservoir
- West Clear Creek, Beaver Creek
- Oak Creek
- East Clear Creek
- Lynx & Watson Lake
- Rim Lakes, Forest Road 300
- Warning! Lakes in the Prescott are high in mercury and may not be suitable for swimming or fishing
- Christopher Creek
- East Verde @ Waterwheel
- River Island
- Big Lake & Buffalo Crossing on the Black River
- Alamo Lake
- Blue River
- Verde River @ Parson TH
- Verde HS - Low water only
- Castle HS - private resort
- Roosevelt, Canyon & Apache Lakes / Salt River
- Lake Pleasant
- Roper HS - State Park
- Hooker HS Nature Conservancy
- Agua Caliente
- Hutch Pool, Romero Pools, Seven Falls - Catalina Mtns
- Patagonia Lake

Riparian : relating to or living on the bank of a natural watercourse such as a river or lake.

The riparian areas along our streams and lakes allow water to nuture our trees and plants, our animals, birds and water creatures. The riparian areas are important as they protect the top soil and allow multiple species to share the area. We should treat the riparian areas with care!

Arizona's people love our rivers and lakes. As the temperatures rise, residents crowd around any body of water to gain relief from the heat, always finding a new twist to enjoy the water.

Fossil Creek

Water Safety Precautions

* Know how to swim!

* Always tell someone where you will be swimming - someone who can summon help if needed.

* Always swim with an adult who knows how to swim well.

* Never dive or jump into water when you do not know the depth or what rocks lie under the surface.

* Do not swim in strong currents.

* Always be aware of weather conditions upstream - get out if there is a danger of flash flooding.

Visit a Dam!

Have you ever visited a dam? Both Hoover Dam and Glen Canyon Dam offer tours for visitors. This is a good way to see how the electricity is made for all our video games.

Parents, this is federal property. Be aware that security precautions do apply.

Colorado River
Glen Canyon Dam / Lake Powell

Colorado River
Hoover Dam / Lake Mead

Colorado River
Davis Dam

Bill Williams River
Alamo Lake & Dam

Colorado River
*Parker
Horsegate
Palo Verde*

Aqua Fria River
*Waddell Dam /
Lake Pleasant*

Colorado River
*Imperial Dam &
Laguna Dam*

Gila River
*Painted Rocks Dam
& Reservoir*

Verde River
*Horseshoe Dam & Reservoir
Bartlett Dam Reservoir & Dam
Granite Reef Diversion Dam*

Salt River
*Theodore Roosevelt Dam / Roosevelt Lake.
Horse Mesa Dam / Apache Lake.
Mormon Flat Dam / Canyon Lake.
Stewart Mountain Dam / Saguaro Lake*

Gila River
Coolidge Dam / San Carlos Lake

Captured Water

Water is one of Arizona's most valuable resources. Let's think about some of the ways we use water.

* Drinking
* Cooking
* Swimming
* Bathing
* Washing clothes
* Growing plants and food
* Cooling off something hot
* Reducing the dust

All these are important ways we use water. We need to use our water wisely so that we will have enough in the dry years. When working in the kitchen and outside we should turn off the water when we are not actively using it.

One way we use water in this state is to supply electricity. We don't have many natural lakes and when we get rain, the water tends to run downstream very fast. Our federal government built huge dams on three of our rivers to create lakes to make electricity and to water our fields.

Come on, while Gavin is dreaming about jumping off waterfalls, let's go check out one of Arizona's dams.

Stop a moment and take a long look at the big cement wall in the photograph. This is a dam that was built across a river bed between two steep cliffs. The dam holds back all the water that flows into the Colorado river, creating Lake Mead. Take a look at the map page and you'll see where lakes were created by dams built decades ago.

To see inside the dam, we have to take a tour. After stepping into an elevator, we drop down, down, down, deep inside the dam. To make electricity, workers inside the dam allow water to flow into big wheels called turbines. As the turbines begin to spin, magnets within the generators creat energy. This energy provides the power flowing into wires that carry electricity to our homes and offices.

When we look at the generators. they seem so big, making the people working near them look small. These machines help give us the electricity we need to run our air conditioners, our lights and all our electronic gear. They serve a very important purpose in our state.

A Crack

Have you tried to build a dam across a stream? What happened? Did the water flow around and over the rocks and sticks you used?

Engineers carefully look at the place where a dam will be built. Is the rock fractured? Is it hard like granite or porous like sandstone?

Throughout Arizona we see canyons where rivers or streams carry rock, dirt and sediment downstream. As a river cuts a channel, steep banks may form on either side of the river, making it more difficult to enter the canyon. Each year more dirt and rock slip into the river's current and the the canyon becomes a little deeper.

Arizona has one of the greatest canyons on the earth. More than just one canyon, the Grand is a whole network of canyons. At the lowest point the Grand Canyon is over a mile deep and at the widest point, eighteen air miles across.

To those standing on the rim, the Colorado River is a slender streak of brown water at the bottom of the canyon. A map reveals that the Colorado River

Looking down the Bright Angel trail toward Indian Gardens.

Opposite page:
Mule Train climbing toward south rim.
Colorado River at Phantom Ranch.

flows from the mountains of Colorado down to the Gulf of Mexico. The canyon is lined with walls of fractured rock. The cracks tell us that more than water worked to create this network of canyons.

Many geologists believe that the river cut through layers of rock as the earth's surface shifted upward. Another group of scientists suggest a shallow

Mule train coming!

in the Earth

inland lake may have widened fractures and existing channels until a catastropic event allowed the water to cut through the uplift, forming the maze of canyons and monuments.

Looking at the canyon walls, we can see layer after layer of rock. Some layers are porous sandstone and others are fine-

Why does the Colorado River appear to be brown instead of green or blue?

While air temperatures at the bottom of the Grand Canyon may be well over 100 degrees during the summer, the river water below Glen Canyon Dam remains around 46 degrees.

grained as silt from a river

People from all over the world come to stand on the edge of the Grand Canyon and hope to see the Colorado River below. Within it's walls, monuments of rock rise from the canyon floor. Side canyons have developed, leaving a maze of rocky passages.

When visiting the rim, look into the canyon and let your eyes find a path to the canyon floor below. In the canyon walls, we see ledges, cliffs and talus piles formed by rock slides. The cliffs appear to be easy to bypass but if we climb down to the red wall formation, we find these cliffs are hundreds of feet high.

Native Americans in this region long ago discovered routes to the river. We find their ruins in the canyon. When early explorers tried to descend to the river, they were stopped by the red wall. The depth and size of the canyon are still an obstacle, requiring hours of road travel to reach the north rim.

Not all visitors settle for the view from the rim. Some choose to hike down into the canyon, others ride the mule train down to Phantom Ranch. Other visitors float down the river, gaining a unique view into earth's history. Can you imagine walking 24 miles along a trail to cross the canyon carrying a backpack with your sleeping bag, clothes and food?

Grand Canyon Facts

Length? From the dam below Lake Powell, following the river to Lake Mead is 277 miles.

Width? In Marble Canyon, the walls are 600 feet apart. Further downstream the width averages around 10 miles, stretching up to 18 miles wide.

Depth? Up to 6000 feet deep, over a mile. The deepest canyon in China drops to 11,000 feet.

North **Rim** is over 8,000 feet in elevation while the South Rim is 7,000 feet. Both Rims have facilities for visitors but only the South rim is open in the winter.

The only **village** inside the the canyon, along the river, is at Phantom Ranch. serving all the hikers and visitors passing through the canyon.

Temperatures range from snowy & cold in the winter on the canyon rim to 60 degrees at the river. The summer warms up to as high as 90 degrees on the rim and 100+ degrees in the inner canyon.

Hiking? There are trails throughout the canyon but the three most popular are the North & South Kaibab along with the Bright Angel. Plan on walking 24 miles to cross from the North to the South Rim.

Swimming? No! The river averages around 46 degrees and swimmers would quickly lose their body heat. The current is also unpredictable. Only trout seem to relish the cool temperature.

National Treasure - The Grand Canyon became a national park in February 1919, just six years after Arizona became a state.

Arizona is riddled with mountains and canyons, leaving us some great places to explore. Canyons are not the only cracks that run through the rock on our earth's surface. Near the town of Page in northern Arizona, Antelope Creek has cut a slot through layers of sandstone into Lake Powell.

Slots are only a few feet wide in places with the rock walls carved into hidden pockets and passages. Water surging through the slot as a flash flood has carved these narrow passages. They are fun to explore.

We should never be in a slot or narrow canyon when rain is falling upstream. Dark clouds upstream and overhead as well as weather reports will warn us of rain coming.

A flash flood develops when too much water enters a streambed quickly. The water sweeps down the stream, growing larger with each yard. When a flash flood rushs through a narrow canyon with vertical walls, there is little time to get out of the way. The water will sweep away anything in its path.

When it is dry, the slots are special places to explore as we look at the beautiful shapes carved into the sandstone walls.

The sandstone walls of Antelope Slot

Green

In the previous pages, we have looked at mountains, caves and waterfalls - all part of the landscape around us. What about trees and animals? And why don't pine trees live in the desert?

Arizona has one of the most diverse climates in the world. Scientists tells us that Arizona has seven ecological zones, based on elevation and the plants and animals that live in each zone.

The earth's surface in Arizona stretches from below sea level up to 12,600 feet. That's over two miles above sea level. This means that temperatures in Arizona can stretch from very hot in the summer in the desert to freezing blizzards in the highlands during the winter.

The plants and animals at different elevations reflect this difference. You won't find the ponderosa pine living in the desert just as rattlesnakes are rare in the highest mountains. The mountains of southern Arizona are given a special name - *sky islands*, meaning that they serve as a refuge for plants and animals that would not normally live in a sea of desert.

Desert hillside with saguaro cactus

& Growing

ecological zone: an area of land that is defined by elevation, the amount of rain and snowfall and the plants and animals that live in the zone.

Ecological Zones of Arizona

Alpine
11,500+ feet
Above tree-line, grass and lichen

Spruce & Fir
8,000-11,500 feet
Aspen, Spruce and Fir trees

Ponderosa
6,500 - 8,000
Ponderosa pine with oak, pinyon and juniper

Transition or Woodland
5,500 - 6,500 feet
Oak, pinyon and juniper

Upper Sonoran
4,000 - 5,500 feet
Higher range woodland with oak, pinyon and juniper
Lower range - grasslands

Lower Sonoran
below 3,500 feet
Desert with mesquite and palo verde trees in the upper range.
Lower range - cacti are prominant.

Cooler

Warmer

Mountain hillside with ponderosa pine

Prickly!

Over 60 species of cactus have adapted to our desert climate. When you look at the spines sprouting from the ribs of a saguaro, you would not think of them as leaves. These narrow sharp spines are leaves that have adapted to a very hot, dry climate. With less surface exposed to the hot temperatures, the cactus spines lose less moisture when it is hot.

If we grab the spines, they pierce our hands. Ouch! These spines also protect the cactus from large predators.

Have you looked closely at the ribs of a saguaro cactus? These expand and and contract with the amount of water stored in the saguaro's tissue. A mature saguaro can store up to 200 gallons of water.

We might think of the thorns on the ocotillo cactus as modified leaves, just like the spines on the cholla. A thorn is defined as a branch that has adapted to desert climate. Observe an ocotillo a week after a rain storm and you will see leaves appear among the thorns. The branches of an ocotillo have long been used for fences in the desert as predators avoid the thorns.

Tohono O'odham people used the fruit of the saguaro, the cholla and the prickly pear for food. Each spring, the women used long sticks to knock the saguaro blossoms and fruit to the ground where they were gathered.

The agave gave native Americans fiber for mats and the pads as food.

cholla, prickly pear and agave

Some trees are deciduous, some evergreen. Do you know the difference?

Evergreen plants keeps their green leaves year round. The palo verde and mesquite are evergreen trees found in the desert. Both have small leaves, reducing the amount of moisture the plant loses in hot weather.

In the woodland zones, we find the evergreen juniper and pinyon pine. Their leaves look very different from what we think of as deciduous trees.

pine   juniper

Why do pine trees have skinny long needles for leaves instead of broad, flat leaves?

Pine needles thrive in higher elevations. Like the thorns of a cactus, the needles are modified leaves, covered with a waxy coating that reduces water loss. Moisture is retained in the center of the needle, protected from freezing temperatures. The needle is less likely to be damaged by snow and ice in our mountain climates.

Look at the difference between the needles of a ponderosa pine and a juniper. Both have a waxy covering to protect them from cold temperatures but they appear very different.

Native Americans still use the berries of the juniper for food and dye.

The pinyon pine gives us pine nuts, a popular snack.

Pinyon and ponderosa pines are evergreen trees that grow on our mountains. Arizona has the largest ponderosa or yellow pine forest in the world. The mature ponderosa smells like vanilla when we lean into the trunk of the tree.

The Desert's Secrets

Cottonwood trees along the Verde River near the town of Cottonwood

Walking across the desert, we see a big shady green tree on the horizon. As we walk closer we realize the tree stands beside a desert wash. What can we learn from that tree?

Cottonwoods are often the marker for a streambed or spring that may have water for a few weeks, or even months, each year. The wind catches the fluffy down protecting the seeds and carries them to damp ground where the seeds can sprout and grow. Cottonwoods make desert gullies beautiful with their green leaves and shade.

Deciduous trees shed their leaves in the winter season.

In the winter months, cottonwood and sycamore lose their leaves. They are classified as deciduous. When out for an adventure, see what other plants you can find that are deciduous.

Arizona is known around the world for the desert wild flowers that bloom each spring. They won't bloom unless we receive rain during the winter months. Just like the cactus, they wait for the moisture before they shine with color across the desert landscape.

High in the mountains, wild flowers appear during the warmer months. They grow from seeds carried by wind to these high elevations.

Slime

Who likes to drag the slimy, green algae up from the bottom of a pond? What good is that slimy stuff?

Many of our lakes show green vegetation growing along the bottom. Algae doesn't just grow under water.

When you see rocks, especially rock cliffs with green or orange lichen, this is a form of algae growing on the surface. The algae tells us that water has been present allowing the algae to grow. During the dry season, the lichen clings to the rock surface until the rainy season returns. Whether in water or on land, algae is an important part of our ecosystem.

The Native Americans harvested wild rice as part of their diet. They developed an early type of corn from a wild grain.

We can harvest the seeds of wild plants and grow new plants. Find a wild flower that has finished blooming and left a small pod. Look very closely at the pod and break it open to find the seeds

Press the seed lightly into a cup of soil. Add a little water to the soil. Every couple of days, add a few drops over the seed and watch to see if it sprouts into a plant. Wildflower seeds are difficult to grow . Transplant the plant outside once it is 4-6 inches tall and water every couple of days.

When does a tree become a rock?

When a tree is buried in mud for a long time, the wood does not decay due to a lack of oxygen. Over time the wood fiber is replaced by silica or calcite which hardens into rock. Arizona has a National Park that displays huge tree trunks of petrified wood.

Plants and trees are not the only life forms that live in our wild places. Arizona has an amazing variety of wildlife that may appear if we quietly observe our surroundings either in the desert and forest.

Animals

Mule deer are usually larger than the Coues whitetail. The Whitetail live in the rocky peaks of our mountain ranges while the mule deer prefers grazing in the meadows of northern Arizona. When a white tail is startled, it's white tail flies up while the mule deer has a black tip to it's tail. Notice the mule deer's long ears.

The antlers of a whitetail have points off the main beam while the main beam of a mule deer antlers will split into two.

Both types of deer have brown hair with white rumps. They will dash off when interrupted, stopping a few yards away to peek back at what scared them.

Photo: Anita Porter

The Rocky Mountain elk that live in our mountains were first brought into Arizona from the state of Wyoming. When settlers first came to this area, Merriam elk bugled through our pines.

The males call the females with a high-pitched squeal. Each winter the elk lose their antlers and begin to grow a new pair that will be ready for sparring with rivals in the fall.

The animals have brown

Hopping, Climbing, Creeping, Slithering

Remember! These are wild animals and we should observe them from a safe distance!

hair and white white rumps. A full grown male will weight around 700 pounds and stand five feet tall at the shoulder. These are big, powerful animals. Do not approach elk if you see the animals feeding along the highway.

The elk on the south rim of the Grand Canyon learned to turn the handles on the water storage tanks for a cool drink. They were not good at turning off the handles and disliked sharing with visitors! Park employees modified the handles.

Deer and elk will run when startled but the pronghorn hop, springing away at the hint of danger. They have a reddish brown coat with a white rump. An adult stands about three feet at the shoulder and weigh between 75-100 pounds.

The pronghorn is the fastest animal in North America, running at 35 miles an hour and faster for short spurts. They live in the grasslands, grazing on grass and keeping an eye on approaching enemies. It is very hard to sneak up on a pronghorn.

It is not unusual for forest visitors to find a baby animal they suspect has been abandoned. They think the parent is gone and the baby is helpless. Picking up the animal, they bring it to the wildlife experts.

Bad Idea!

Chances are good that the parent is not far from the baby animal and will return once we leave the area.

Experts warn us to leave baby animals alone. Do not touch! Do not move them! If you are concerned, call Game and Fish to report what you have seen.

Meet two White-tail Coues Fawns

Baby fawns are born with spots that help disguise them in the underbrush. Their mother will hide them while she is grazing nearby.

For the first two weeks, the fawns have no scent which helps protect them from predators. After four or five days, the fawns are ready to jump up and run if a predator comes near.

Sometimes female deer are killed on our highways. What happens to the fawns when their mother is gone?

In the summer of 2018 Pat and Randy at the Grand Canyon Deer Farm adopted two orphan white-tail deer. Due to an accident, their mother could no longer care for them. Pat fed the fawns goat's milk and kept them in a special pen. Just like babies, these fawns loved their bottles - every three hours, night and day!

Thank you to the owners and staff of the Deer Farm for the up close view of the fawns and other animals. Hours 9-5, are extended during the summer months. The Deer Farm is located just off I-40 at the exit #171, east of Williams, AZ. Check out the Deer Farm on facebook for recent photos.

Desert big horn sheep have adapted to living in the mountains of Arizona and New Mexico. They can weigh up to 275 pounds with hooves that are flexible and cupped to help them grip steep, rocky surfaces.

Part of the year, the males will fight over the females by charging a competitor. Their horns curl, reaching up to three feet in length. They favor wild grass but have been known to break open a cactus to savor the moist fiber inside.

A bison, once native to the plains, now in Arizona

Black bears still roam our mountains, sometimes dropping into town for a visit during a drought. A full-grown male black bear stands four feet at the shoulder and weights about 220 pounds. If the bear should stand on his back two legs, he would be closer to six feet tall. The female black bear has one or two cubs in mid winter. They stick close to their mother for the first few months, learning to survive.

A bear cannot retract his claws like a cat. The claws are always available to rip open a tree or turn over a rock as the bear looks for tasty grubs. Bears like berries for dessert.

A bear can run 40 miles an hour for short distances. If you should meet a black bear try to scare him by waving your arms and making a lot of noise.

Bobcats, a member of the lynx family, are found throughout the desert and foothill regions of the state. Weighing up to 30 pounds and 24 inches long, they are only a little larger than a house cat. Their speckled coats blend into the ground cover as they stalk their prey. Five-inch-long ears sport little tuffs of hair on the tips.

While walking their claws are retracted The claws are unsheathed when they bring down their prey. Bobcats have adapted to urban settings, making dens under porches and in sheds. When rodents are not available, they may hunt small pets for their dinner.

The Mountain Lion, called a cougar or puma, is the largest cat in Arizona. They often have dens in mountain cliffs where they can keep an eye on what moves below them. An adult cat could stand three feet at the shoulder and weigh up to 220 pounds. Just like your pet cat, they can sheath their claws.

Cats prefer to attack from ambush and the mountain lion will circle its prey. They jump on the back of the prey, biting the neck. Never turn your back on a mountain lion. Mountain lions are beautiful to watch as they move along the cliffs and through the forest.

The beautiful skin of a jaguar seems to be patterned with fingerprints. Jaguar have been returning to Arizona from Mexico after being absent for decades. They are powerful cats that hunt during the night. They can be identified by the pattern of their spots.

A large male can weigh up to 340 pounds, and be six feet from the nose to the base of his tail. In watching a jaguar drag a deer carcass into the brush, we see how powerful the muscles are in this cat.

The ring-tail cat, a member of the raccoon family, is much smaller than a mountain lion. As our state's mammal, they live in rocky, dry places, hunting for small rodents. They might visit your camp at night, peeping down from a tree, to see what food scraps you've left. Their big eyes take in every detail, including the s'more you're making.

Like the raccoon, they have a long tail that allows them to balance in tight places. The raccoon's mask gives him away every time. As cute as a raccoon may be, never try to pet one as they can give a nasty bite.

Photo: National Park Service

The raccoon will be happy to raid your bird feeder.

Some visitors might think a coatimundi is related to a bear but like the ringtail cat, they are members of the raccoon family. A coatimundi isn't picky about what he eats, whether berries and plants or small rodents and grasshoppers. He loves a warm egg.

In southern Arizona, Monkey spring is named for a family of coatmundis that lived nearby. They are very social animals and fun to watch as they scurry about, poking their long noses into everything.

An adult male can be 25 inches long and weigh up to 13 pounds. They use their long tail to help them balance when climbing trees but they are usually found running along the ground.

Coatis are most often found in the foothills of southern Arizona.

^ Badgers have wide bodies with short legs. Their triangle-shaped faces end in a long snout. Their paws have long claws that help them dig in pursuit of small rodents. Badgers are known to be fierce fighters when attacked by a larger animal.

The badger may hunt at night but in remote areas will be active during the day. When running across open terrain, their bodies seem to ripple over their legs.

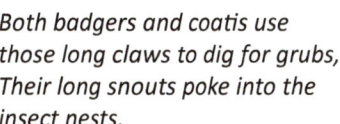

Thank you to Bearizona, located in Williams, as they share their bears and other mammals.

Both badgers and coatis use those long claws to dig for grubs, Their long snouts poke into the insect nests.

This is NOT your dog!

< Gray Fox, Photo: National Park Service

^ Coyote

For children, a coyote may be a favorite cartoon character. The real life canines are a study in learning to adapt to their territory whether in the mountains or the desert. Both the coyote and the fox are stealthy animals living in rural and urban settings, surviving on the food sources available. The average coyote is 2-3 feet tall, 40 inches in length, weighing about 35 pounds with a light brown coat. The gray fox is smaller than a coyote, weighing about 20 pounds. They are curious and like to watch people from a distance. Note this fox's sharp ears and watchful eyes.

Javelinas, or peccaries, are social animals living in packs. Adults are about 30 inches long and weigh up to 85 pounds. As omnivores, they seek roots, grasses, seeds and fruit. A Halloween pumpkin might be just the treat they are seeking if they visit your house! As our climate warms, peccaries are moving higher in elevation. They are not hesitant to invade an urban setting for food.

You will probably never see a river otter in the wild in Arizona but a few remain, sliding down slick muddy banks into our rivers. Their habitat has shrunk as more people move into Arizona and live along our rivers. They love playing in the water but their real interest is catching a fish for dinner.

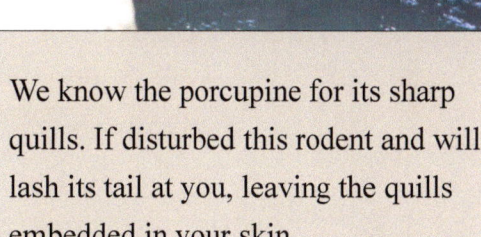

Photo: National Park Service

Beavers live in our streams, too. They are known to build lodges out of trees they chew with their their long front teeth. If they didn't chew their teeth would not stop growing. If you see a dense pile of logs next to a pool of water, look carefully. It could be a beaver lodge with an underwater entrance. You are not an invited visitor!

We know the porcupine for its sharp quills. If disturbed this rodent and will lash its tail at you, leaving the quills embedded in your skin.

Under the needles, the porcupine has a small round body and small ears. Neither the face or the pads of the feet have the long hairs we know as quills. The quills inflate as they strike their victim, sinking deeper into warm flesh.

Native Americans used quills in making jewelry, clipping the ends to deflate the hollow tube. Keep your dog away from a porcupine as the dog is convinced that with the next fight, he will win. The dog never wins and comes away with a mouth full of quills.

chipmunk

squirrel

Like squirrels and chipmunks, the prairie dog is a member of the rodent family. As a keystone species, 36 other species depend on or live around the dogs' complex tunnel system. The light brown rodents sit on their back haunches near a tunnel entrance, watching for predators. They warn other dogs of a predator with a high pitched chirp.

Prairie Dog / Photos: National Park Service

The kangaroo rat, related to the pocket gopher, has adapted to our desert climate. He hops from place to place, looking for seeds and insects. The bottom of his feet are insulated with fur. He sleeps in his burrow during hot daytime temperatures, coming out after dark. His large eyes help him to see in the dark and his tiny ears keep him from losing too much water when it is hot.

Kangaroo Rat / Photos: National Park

The desert tortoise can live to be very old, roaming our dry, hot deserts. They feast on the sprigs of grass that emerge from the rocky soil. Like the rodents, their homes are burrows in the sand. In recent years, there has been concern that the horses and cattle are competing with the tortoise for the grass in their common diets.

Photo: National Park Service

Signs of Life Around us

You're walking along a stream. In front of you is a big ol' print from some kind of animal. Is it a bear? No! What do we do?

Stop - Look - Listen

We can learn a lot from the signs that animals leave. One of these prints is from an elk, the other a bear. What differences do you see?

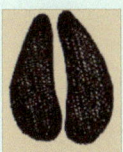 

A bear's claws cannot be retracted so his claws leave a point. The bear's print is completely different from an animal with a hoof like an elk. The elk runs from danger while the bear may put up a fight or may wander away from a threat.

A quarter shows us the size of this elk print.

An old tree trunk gives us another sign. Who left this mark? How was it made? If you guess that an animal with sharp teeth gnawed on this tree, you would be right. The trunk is fairly big so it could not have been a small animal like a squirrel. If you guess a beaver, you would be right.

Another sign for an animal that lives in water is to check whether a paw print is webbed between the toes or just individual toe prints. Both beaver and otter have webbed feet.

How can you tell the difference between a bobcat print and a coyote print? Remember a cat can retract its claws while the dog cannot. Another clue? You can draw an X between a dog's toes and the pad of its paw.

cat   dog

When you have the opportunity, wander along a stream bank and look carefully for prints in the soft earth. The soft ground is the best place to find prints of the animals who live near the stream.

When we are out for a walk, we should stop and look around. If we close our eyes and listen carefully we will hear quiet sounds we often ignore. Whether a sound, a gnawed stick, animal scat or an animal print, these signs give us a different understanding on the world around us.

Rodents, including mice, chipmunks and squirrels, are the favorite food of hawks and owls. Both species hunt for their dinner, silently dropping down on their prey..

Photo: National Park Service

Owls have special feathers that allow them to swoop silently through the forest. As the owls swallow their prey whole, they often spit up chunks of bone and feathers, leaving them for us to find on the ground. Owls can turn their heads 180 degrees and back again to check if we are a threat. Their eyes have special cells that allow them to see very well at night.

Turkey vultures and red-tail hawks are commonly seen across Arizona's skies while the Harris hawk is found only in southern Arizona.

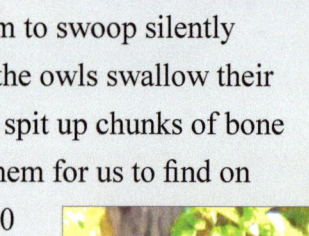

Two other raptors, the eagles and condors, are larger than a hawk. Eagles love to nest around bodies of water where they can fish. Condors, who feed on carrion, have been re-introduced north of the Grand Canyon. They have one of the longest wing spans in North America.

The caracara, part of the falcon family, can be found walking along

Photo: Mike Gilliland

Cactus Wren, our state bird, builds a nest in the saguaros, avoiding the sharp needles on the ribs of the cactus.

Photo: National Park Service

When temperatures turn cold, hummingbirds migrate south into Mexico. During the spring, they return to live in the mountains of Arizona. Their wings move up to 70 times a second, which allows them to dart swiftly from flower to flower and fight other birds that seek the same nectar.

the ground in southern Arizona, turning over rocks, looking for a morsel to eat.

Herons are found along the shores of our lakes. They stand motionless, waiting for a fish to come within striking range.

Ravens, the big black birds we see soaring the wind currents, are scavengers like the condors. They help remove dead animals from our roads. Like the turkey vultures, they can hang almost motionless on hot air thermals. Adult ravens teach their young acrobatic tricks as they ride the wind currents.

These are just a few of the notable birds that live in Arizona. Bird Watchers find a pair of binoculars helpful along with a bird book. A bird feeder and bird bath will bring a number of species to your doorstep.

Photo: National Park Service

"Hey, Dad! Did you forget the rattlesnakes?"

"Gavin, did you know we have 13 different species of rattlesnakes in Arizona? All poisonous!"

"I remember that snake we found under the bush in our back yard."

"Gavin, that's why we always look before we put our hands anyplace. Rattlesnakes aren't the only poisonous snake in Arizona. What about the snake in this photo?

'Red and yellow, can kill a fellow; Red and black, friend of Jack.'

"The red and black bands are next to each other. That's a King snake, Dad! If the red and yellow stripes were next to each other then this would be a coral snake and its bite is deadly. Either way, I would rather just look at the snake and not touch him."

"I think that is a safe plan. How did you learn about the color pattern?"

"People from the Game and Fish Department came to school and taught us about snakes. They showed us a scorpion, too. The bark scorpion is really poisonous."

"Since you know so much about snakes, do you know the difference between the Chuckwalla and the Gila Monster lizards?"

The Chuckwalla or 'desert iguana' resembles a Gila Monster but is not poisonous. He can inflate his middle when squeezing into cracks under big rocks, making it hard for a predator to pull him out for dinner. Adults can reach 18 inches long when mature.

The Gila Monster is thicker around his middle, slower moving and has a beaded look with red and gray coloring. He reaches 24 inches in length and is poisonous! If bitten, it is important to remove the lizard from contact as quickly as possible or he will continue to inject venom.

"Dad, I have friends who talk about hunting and how the meat feeds their families. Can you just go out and shoot a deer?"

"Gavin, Arizona has a lot of rules for hunting deer and elk. Many years ago, people noticed there weren't many animals left. They set rules for when and where we could hunt. This has allowed the animal population to increase in the forests and deserts of our states."

"What about fishing?"

"There is a department that handles the licenses for hunting and fishing. Did you know that the state of Arizona raises fish to stock our lakes and rivers?"

National Fish Hatchery	Arizona Fish Hatcheries
Alchesay-Williams Creek	Sterling Springs Page Springs Tonto Creek Canyon Creek Silver Creek

"How do they do that, Dad?"

"We have fish hatcheries in our state. The hatcheries have big tanks of water. Once the fish hatch from eggs, they are put in the tanks to grow. When the fish are big enough to be caught, men release the fish into a local lake or river."

"How do they get the fish in the water?"

"They just back up to the water's edge and open a door in big tank. The water gushes out of the tank and with the water come the fish."

"They just drop the fish into the lake?"

"That's right. The fish adjust to their new home with lots of bugs to eat and new places to hide from the fishermen."

"Dad, let's get our fishing poles and see what we can catch!"

Ruins
Old, Old Houses

"Dad, I've really had a good time exploring but I've noticed there are only a few people in some of the places we've visited."

"Gavin, let's think back to a time before there were cars, before there were roads. Think back before people built houses like we live in today. What do you think Arizona was like then?"

"Back before people came? I think the trees and grass grew without getting run over. The elk and the deer ate the grass. Maybe something hunted the animals but it wasn't people."

"You know, we can see signs of people who lived here long before roads and cars and houses made out of cement blocks."

"What signs? Where?"

"Gavin, take a look at these rocks. Ancient people carved symbols into the patina on the rock. What do you think they are saying?"

"I see one that looks like an animal with four legs. Was that a dog?"

"More likely a deer. A hunter may have carved that one. Look at this symbol with two legs. Is that you?"

"Funny, dad. How about this circle

Petroglyphs are drawings etched in granite by ancient people. Can you guess what the images mean?
Painted Rock State Park

with the spiral in the middle?"

"We're not sure what that sign indicated. Some people say it is the sign for time that goes on forever. Others say it is related to the sun."

"Why did they scratch these drawings onto the rock?"

"Why did you paint the picture on our refrigerator?"

"Mom told me to paint since I was bored."

"This artist might have been bored or he wanted to remember something special that happened here."

"When humans first came to the southwest, there were no stores, no houses, no roads. Nothing. Look around you! What would you use to build a place to live?"

"Uh, rocks, maybe?"

"How about mud?"

Mud?

"Yeah, mud and rocks stacked into walls. The people used mud to fill the gaps between the rocks."

"Are these houses still around?"

"Some of them have been preserved and we can visit the sites. Come on! Let's take a look."

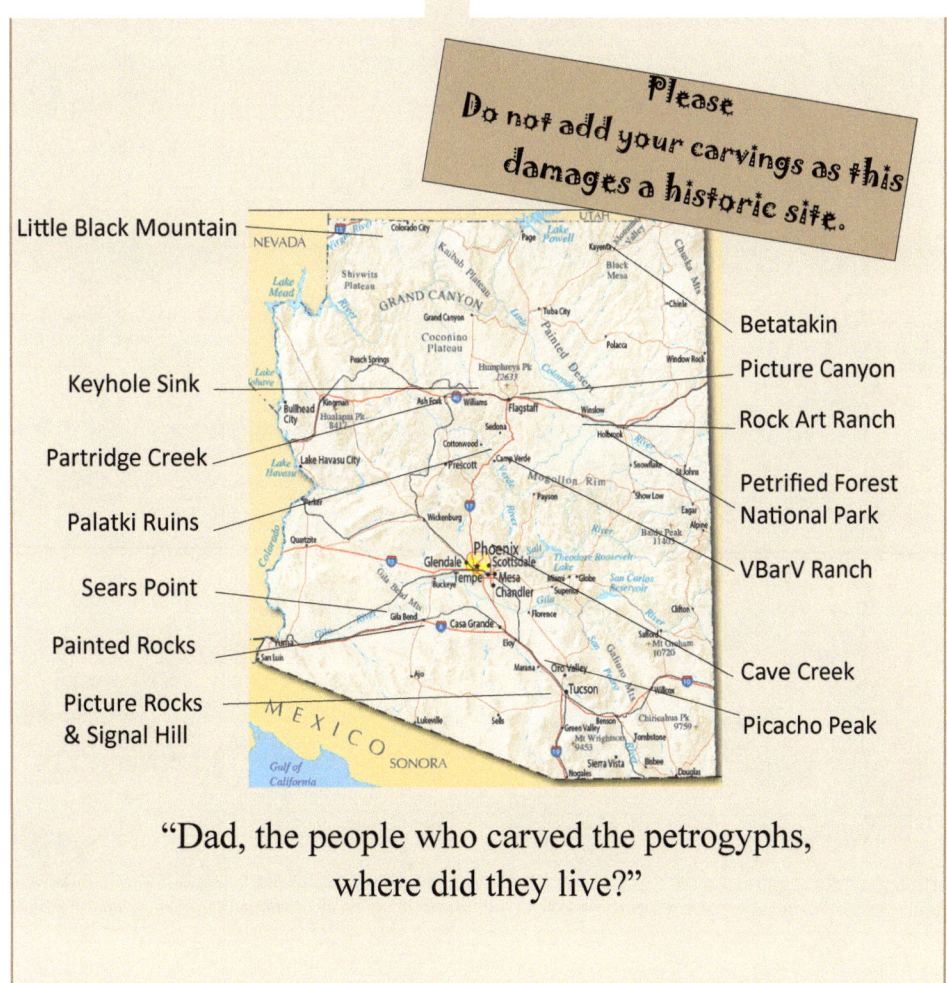

Please Do not add your carvings as this damages a historic site.

"Dad, the people who carved the petrogyphs, where did they live?"

"Gavin, Early native Americans lived in houses built from the materials they found around them: Rocks, sticks and mud. What kind of house would you want to live in?"

Apache brush house

ruins of an ancient pit house

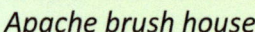

Wupatki pueblo

"What skills would they have needed to live? How would they have found food. How would they build homes? How would they have kept warm in the winter?"

modern hogan

Betatakin cliff dwelling

The ancient people who once lived in Arizona built shelters over shallow pits as their homes. Today, shallow depressions remain from these pit houses, allowing us to use our imagination.

The Apaches were a nomadic tribe that moved frequently living in shelters made of brush.

At Betatakin, early native Americans built their homes along ledges overlooking the canyon. They reached the ledges using ladders from the canyon bottom.

Ropes made of yucca fiber hung down from the cliff edge allowing the men to climb down using footholds.

The people planted gardens along the stream below. They carried water in clay pots back to their homes. Their enemies could not reach them on the high ledges.

Those living in pueblos like the one at Wupatki, had no doors or windows on the first level. They entered the pueblo using a ladder to the second level which could be pulled up when they were attacked.

"Gavin, in southern Arizona ancient people built homes using sticks and brush. In northern Arizona the early Americans built their homes on ledges using rock and mud. In our arid plains, native people built multi-level homes out of rock, using mud as mortar between the slabs. Some pueblos rose as high as three levels.

Do you see any doors on the lowest level? In defending their homes, the builders did not build doors or windows in the lowest level. Those living in the pueblos used ladders to get up to the roof of the first story where they entered their homes. If an enemy attacked, they pulled up the ladder so the enemy could not get into their homes."

"Dad, let's walk down to those walls below the pueblo."

"Gavin, what have you found?"

"Dad, this hole has air blowing out. What is it?"

"Under the ground there are secret passages in the rocks. Sometimes the air flows into the passages and at other times the air flows out. Here, place your hand over this vent. What do you feel?"

"I can feel the air moving. How does it know when to flow in or flow out?"

"As the earth's surface cools or heats up, air flows along the passages. The air pressure also effects the flow of air."

"Come on, I want to show you something else that is really awesome. What do you see below the ruins?"

"There's a big round space surrounded by a low wall. What is it?"

"This was a ball court."

"What ball game did they play?"

"When the ball was tossed into the court between two teams, they would use any surface on their body to hit the ball, except their hands, like we play soccer today. Their goal was to get the ball through a ring on the wall above the court. Everyone in the pueblo would turn out to watch. And, I'm sure there were people who bet on which team would win the game."

"You got a ball, Dad? Can we try this?"

Most likely they joined groups of people living to the south and east of Wupatki. The Sinagua were not the only people that lived in Arizona so long ago. We find ruins from other people groups in the mountains and deserts across or state."

"Are these ancient people related to the native tribes that live here today?"

"The Hopis say the people who once lived in the northeast part of our state are their ancestors, the Hisat'sinom. The Nava-

Wupatki pueblo and ball court with natural blow hole.

"We're out of soccer balls, Gavin. No game today."

"What happened to the people who built this place?"

"This ruin is called Wupatki. It was built by a people called the *Sinagua* around 1,000 years ago. We're not sure why they left, Gavin. One idea is that a long drought came and the people left to find a new home close to a permanent source of water.

jo called this ancient people, the Anasazi. Tohono O'odham people down in the southern part of our state say their ancestors are the Hohokam. Both the Hopis and the Tohono O'oham say they have been here since time immemorial, meaning before anyone can remember or kept records of what was happening. Just like all our other discoveries, people are an important part of Arizona, both past and present.

Over the centuries, just as the land beneath our feet can change, so the people who lived in this region became the tribes we know today: the Hopi, the Pima, the Yavapai and the Tohono O'odham. The Navajo and Apache moved into this region around the same time that other cultures began to move into Arizona.

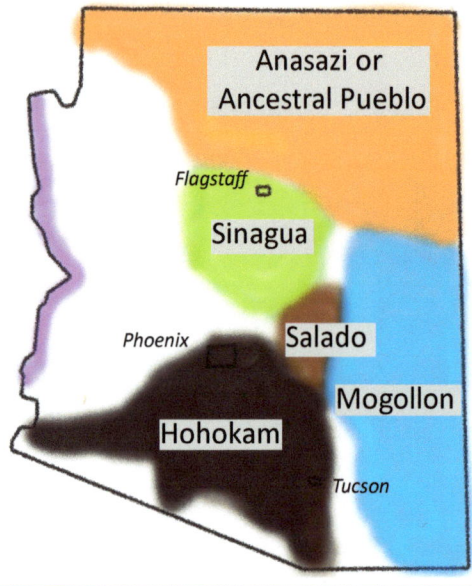

Long before white settlers came to Arizona, ancient people lived in regions across this arid territory. Each region traded with the other regions. Traders brought sea shells and parrot feathers from the coastline of the Gulf of California to the prehistoric people of central Arizona?

Five hundred years ago, Spanish speaking people sailed across the Atlantic and entered North America. Over the next 100 years they would move north from Mexico into what would become southern Arizona, bringing beliefs and culture different from the tribes that were here.

Two hundred years after the Spanish arrived, white settlers began to enter Arizona, coming from the states in the southern part of our country. Others came south from the state of Utah. Each of these groups were seeking new places to live where they could build homes and businesses.

Both the Spanish and white settlers brought cattle into Arizona. They planted crops to feed the cattle and their families.

The native people did not claim small pieces of land for their homes as the white settlers did. Due to fear and misunderstanding the native and white people came into conflict and often fought each other over the rights to land, to water and the right to live as they chose.

Fort Bowie in the Chiricahua Mountains of southern Arizona was one place that the conflict raged over a spring of water. Apache Pass, where Fort Bowie is located, was the site of a famous battle between the Apaches and the United

Native Tribes claim land across Arizona. The U.S. Government recognizes the tribes as sovereign, independent governments located on designated reservations. While reservation land may not be as extensive as the tribe once roamed, many of the tribal members either live on thir ancestral lands or return for special events.

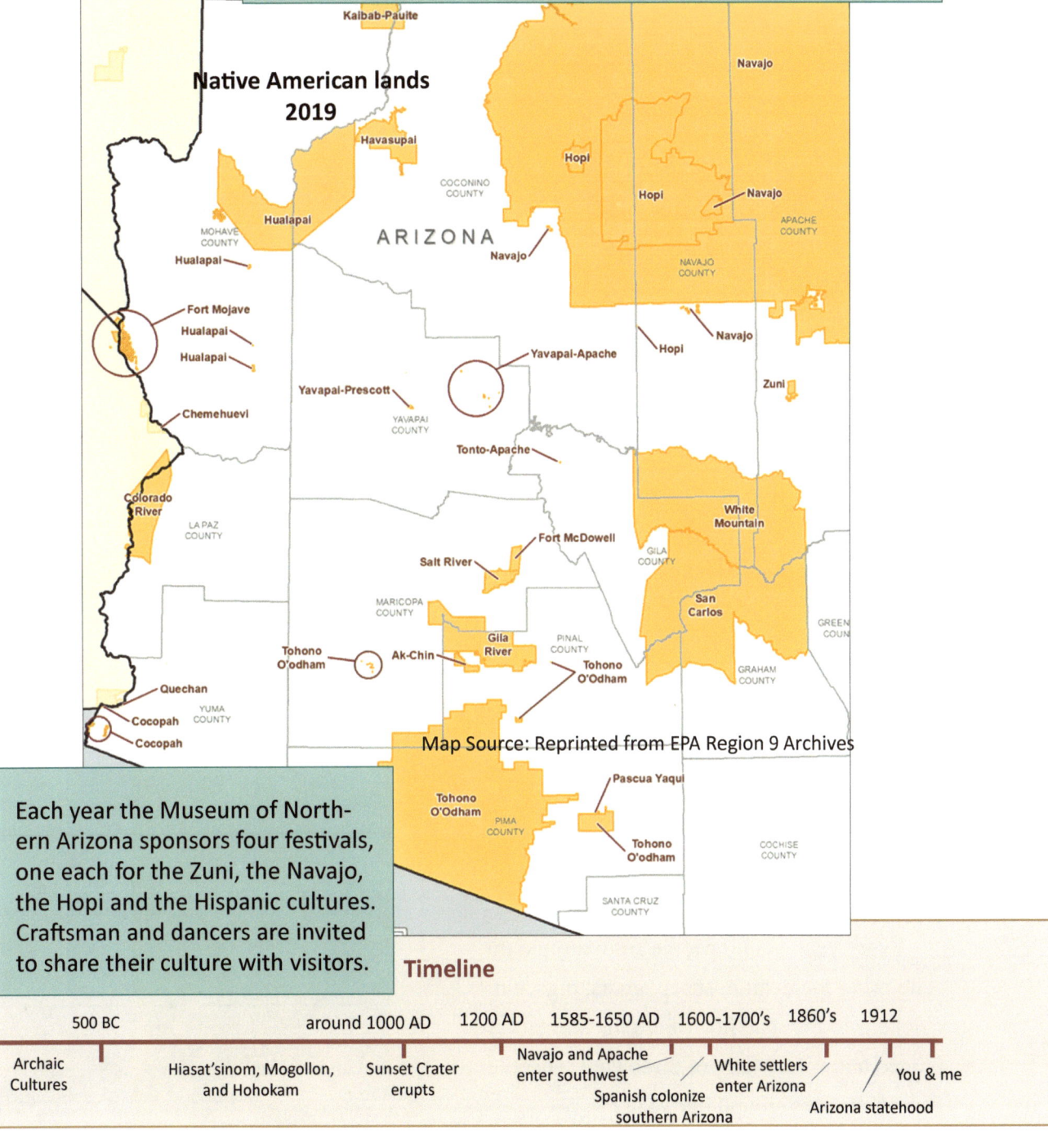

Map Source: Reprinted from EPA Region 9 Archives

Each year the Museum of Northern Arizona sponsors four festivals, one each for the Zuni, the Navajo, the Hopi and the Hispanic cultures. Craftsman and dancers are invited to share their culture with visitors.

Timeline

500 BC	around 1000 AD	1200 AD	1585-1650 AD	1600-1700's	1860's	1912
Archaic Cultures	Hiasat'sinom, Mogollon, and Hohokam	Sunset Crater erupts	Navajo and Apache enter southwest / Spanish colonize southern Arizona	White settlers enter Arizona	Arizona statehood	You & me

States Cavalry. One of the Apache clans had been raiding the ranches in southern Arizona.

A Cavalry Troop stopped at the spring on a patrol following Southern troops during the War Between the States. The Apaches had decided the white people could not use this spring as the tribe relied on this water. The Apaches hid in the hills above the spring and waited for the Cavaly to come to the spring, ambushing the soldiers.

After the battle, the Cavalry built Fort Bowie to defend the route through Apache Pass. They built forts across Arizona to protect the white settlers. This was common in the conflict between the two cultures. The Apache, Navajo and Yavapai tribes were pushed onto reservations where many live today. These reservations have their own government and laws.

For the white and Hispanic settlers, cattle and cotton farming became important industries for many years. For a time, those living in the eastern states thought of Arizona as 'cowboy country.'

We still have cattle and cowboys in our state. These men ride through our wild country, working with cows on the open range. Near Flagstaff, you might even find the cowboys driving the cattle across a major state highway each spring and fall as the herds are moved to their seasonal pastures.

Every year, young people from around the state bring their cattle, sheep, goats, pigs and chickens to the state fair where the animals are judged and sold. Many of these young people live on ranches around our state.

Walnut Canyon / Sinagua

Montezuma Castle / Sinagua

Palatki, Honandi & Tuzigoot ruins / Sinagua

Tonto Cliff Dwelling / Salado

Kinlichee/ Anasazi

Betatakin Anasazi / Ancestral Pueblo

White House Ruin Anasazi / Ancestral Pueblo

Prehistoric Native Ruins

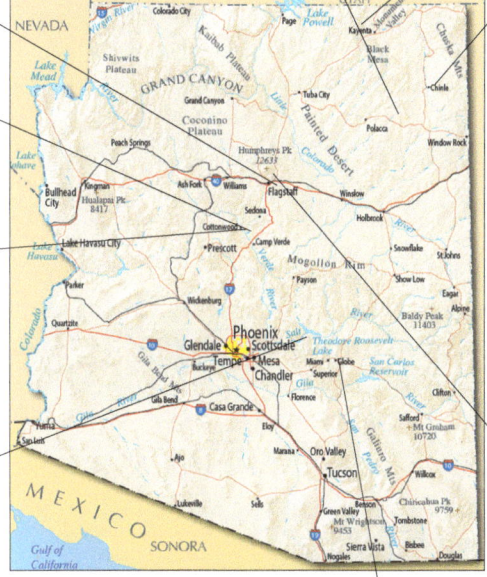

Wupatki/ Sinagua

Besh Ba Gowah Salado

A cowboy pushes a mother and colt into the auction ring on a northern Arizona ranch.

**Arizona claims five 'C's in the the state motto:
Copper, Cattle, Cotton, Climate and Citrus.
These five economic factors help build the economy of our state.**

Playing in the Mud

Do you want to try making your own mud bricks like the Spanish used in their adobe walls? Grab a one-gallon-plastic milk container. Cut off the top of the jug about 5 inches from the bottom.

Mix together:
    2 cups of dirt
  2 big handfuls of straw or dry grass
    1 cup of sand in a bucket.

Add one cup of water and stir. Add a little water at a time until dirt is wet, not soupy.

Spray the inside of the milk carton with cooking spray and pour the mix into the milk carton. Allow the mud to dry for several days.

Flip out the brick onto the ground, tapping the bottom firmly. Making enough bricks for a home take weeks of hard work.

You'll just need a bit more dirt, straw and water to make mortar between each of your bricks.

Like any place, the good guys, the bad guys, men who broke the law, are all part of our history. In the early days of our state's history, those who broke the law were sent to the Territorial Prison in Yuma.

We can visit this historic site in the southwestern corner of our state. The prisoners worked through the heat of the day, breaking rocks. At night bed bugs crawled out of the seams of their mattresses, biting them. Those who broke the rules went to the dark cell. Imagine what it was like to work and live in the desert without air conditioning. The last place you wanted to go was the Territorial prison.

Yuma was an important crossing on the Colorado River that marked the western boundary of our state. We've come along way as we've explored Arizona.

The bars and cells of Yuma Territorial Prison.

If you were moving to an unsettled place, with no houses, no grocery stores or gas stations, not even roads. What would you take with you?

In the 1800's, the early settlers brought only what would fit into a small wagon: Food, a change of clothes, a few tools, some seeds and their weapons. They built their homes with the tools, cleared ground, hoping to grow enough food to get them through the winter months.

The smallest accidents could cost a life if infection set in. There was danger from animals and from hostile native Americans. The frontier was not a friendly place when the first settlers arrived.

Those who settled in the Valley of the Sun, lived without air conditioning or even evaporative coolers, in temperatures over 100 degrees. In the north country, the only source of heat was a fire in the fireplace or wood stove. Each family had to cut their own wood or buy coal. With no electricity to run refrigerators, food was kept cool in root cellars. Clothes were washed in a big tub over an open fire.

Just like the ruins of the native Americans, we find the ruins of small towns and settlements throughout Arizona. Some of the old places like Yuma Territorial Prison have been restored as State Parks. Others are nothing more than a handful of dilapidated buildings exposed to sun, wind and rain. We might once again ask Gavin, "What house would you like to live in?"

A fortified ranch home founded by the LDS that supplied cheese and meat to merchants as far away as Salt Lake City.

Windsor Castle & Pipe Springs National Monument

The site of a Spanish Presidio founded in 1752 to protect the Spanish settlers.

Tubac & Tumacacori

Founded in 1881, Fairbank was a railroad camp for the mining industry.

Fairbank

The ranch first belonged to John & Emma Lee who ran a ferry across the Colorado River.
Photo: Betty Russell

Lonely Dell Ranch

Established in 1865, Fort Verde is a former US Army camp in reponse to conflict between the Yavapai Indians and white settlers.

Homes in the 1800s

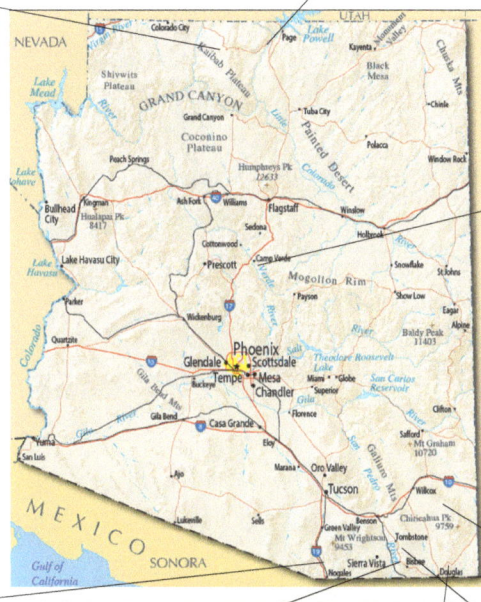

Fort Verde

Fort Bowie

Miltary Camp established 1862-1894 by the California volunteers to guard against attacks b the Apaches.

Fort Rucker

Former US Army post in 1880-1890s, established for the conflict with the Apache tribe and the lawlessness of the border region.

Tombstone

Mining town founded in 1879 by Ed Schefflin, near site of several mines.

"Gavin, what do you think the best part of Arizona is when we're outdoors?"

"I like playing in the water a lot. Sometimes, I like climbing mountains, too. I can see a long way. What do you think is the best, Dad?"

"Gavin, I would say that I just enjoy doing or going some special places as a family."

"What? I thought you meant a place or something to do."

One Special Place

"Gavin, back about one hundred years ago, some men got together and decided that there were places in the United States that were very special. They wanted to preserve those special places for everyone to enjoy. They set aside the places that were so special. I'm talking about our national parks and state parks where everyone is allowed to visit.

It doesn't matter how much money you make or what kind of car you drive, where you live or what job you do. This is our land, set aside for us to enjoy."

"That is special, Dad. Where are these places?"

"Let's take a look, Gavin."

West Clear Creek

In 1895, the federal government in Washington, DC began to set aside some beautiful places for everyone to enjoy. By setting them aside, that meant that no one could come in and build a city on top of that beautiful place. Today we call these special places National Parks. The state of Arizona, in fact all fifty states, set aside land as State Parks as well.

Look these Parks up online!

- Parashant-Vermillion Cliffs NM
- Lake Powell & Glen Canyon NM
- Pipe Spring
- Navajo NM
- Grand Canyon NP
- Wupatki & Sunset Crater NMs
- Walnut Canyon NM
- Canyon de Chelly NM
- Montezuma Castle & Well
- Hubbell Trading Post HS
- Tuzigoot NM
- Petrified Forest NP
- Agua Fria NM
- Tonto NM
- Casa Grande Ruins NM
- Saguaro NP
- Fort Bowie HS
- Chiricahua NM
- Organ Pipe NM
- Coronado NM
- Tumacacori HP

In 1905, President Teddy Roosevelt set aside land around Yosemite Valley in California as our first National Park. The the Grand Canyon was designated as a national park in 1919. Today, Arizona has three National Parks, four National Monuments and 17 National Recreation Areas. All of these are set aside for people you and me to enjoy.

NM - National Monument
NP - National Park
HS = Historic Site

State Parks in Arizona

Mountain Central
Dead Horse Ranch State Park
Fort Verde State Historic Park
Granite Mountain Hotshots Memorial State Park
Jerome State Historic Park
McFarland State Historic Park
Red Rock State Park
Riordan Mansion State Historic Park
Rockin' River Ranch State Park
Slide Rock State Park
Tonto Natural Bridge State Park
Verde River Greenway State Natural Area

Tubac Presidio: History

Slaughter's Ranch: Western history and natural springs

Colorado River
Alamo Lake State Park
Buckskin Mountain State Park
Cattail Cove State Park
Havasu Riviera State Park
Lake Havasu State Park
River Island State Park
Yuma Quartermaster Depot State Historic Park
Yuma Territorial Prison State Historic Park

Casa Grande National Monument: Ancient people

Find all these state parks online and learn more about what unique opportunities each offers.

Slide Rock and the Verde River Greenway

Northeast
Homolovi State Park
Lyman Lake State Park

Central
Boyce Thompson Arboretum State Park
Lost Dutchman State Park

Southeast
Catalina State Park
Dankworth Pond State Park
Kartchner Caverns State Park
Oracle State Park
Patagonia Lake State Park
Picacho Peak State Park
Roper Lake State Park
San Rafael State Natural Area
Sonoita Creek State Natural Area
Tombstone Courthouse State Historic Park
Tubac Presidio Historic Park

Roper Lake: Natural hot tub

"Dad, There are so many places we can explore."

"Ok, Gavin. But first, I have a question for you?"

"Yeah, Dad?"

"Did you find an adventure in the places we visited?"

"More than an adventure! Dad, I found caves and waterfalls. I found old ruins and volcanoes that don't explode anymore! And I found time with you! Arizona is a great place to explore!"

Lovin' the Outdoors

The outdoor adventures
we did not talk about:

Fly a kite
Moonlight walks with a flashlight
Science-based Kits (National Geographic or Edmund Scientific)
Gardening
Build a fort
Building roads in the sandbox, castles in the sand.
Toy boat sailing
Picnic in the desert or on a hilltop
Scavenger or treasure hunt
Camping start in the back yard, later move on to a campground.
Flashlight Tag
Cooking outdoors (BBQ, solar oven)
Hiking / outdoor exploration
Canoeing / Kayaking on flat water
Star-gazing at a local Observatory
Tree climbing
Rock climbing
Rocket Building
Sidewalk Chalk drawings

Explore a creek, identify animal foot prints
Explore a creek & identify animal foot prints
Build a dam
Dance through a sprinkler
Water fight
Make leaf etchings
Build a bug village
Wash your parents' car
Wash the dog
Puddle jump
Roll down a hill - move obstacles, sticks and rocks first
Catch a frog (then, let it go)
Make a rock cairn - rock balancing
Make a slip-and-slide with plastic, dish detergent and a water hose.
Nerf gun fight
Create an obstacle course and time each entrant
Flashlight hike at night

> Apple Picking,
> Corn Picking,
> Pumpkin gathering
> By all means,
> avoid cotton picking!

Organized sports:

T-ball / baseball / softball
Soccer
Flag Football

Back yard bowling with water bottles & a plastic ball
Bike ride
Try an aerial ropes course
Make ice cream
Watermelon seed spitting contest
Apple bobbing
Go to a playground / park
Roast marshmellows over a campfire (adult supervision required!)
Build a drum - drum circle with friends
Photography walk - requires a camera
Build a marble course with foam noodles and milk cartons.
Got a dog? Teach the dog a trick
Create a May-pole with friends
Roller skate or rollerblade

Visit an arboretum in Flagstaff, Globe or near the *Phoenix Zoo*

Star-gazing at a local *Observatory*

Visit a *Zoo* or *Wildlife Center*

Skyride at the *Arizona Snowbowl*

Game & Fish Outdoor Exposition

Science in the Park (multiple cities)

Outdoor Games:
Tag (including freeze tag & tunnel tag)
Four Square
Hopscotch
Badminton
Croquet
Horseshoes
Bolo Toss
Miniature Golf
Corn Hole
Frisbee catch or Frisbee golf
Capture the Flag
(Avoid lawn darts)

A note to the responsible adult: This book does not contain directions to the landforms and other features we've discussed. Most adults now carry a cellular phone with access to the internet. All of these features are listed on google maps. Before you leave home, copy the instructions as some back country regions in Arizona do not have access to the internet. It is not good to find yourself lost without an online map to guide you to civilization.

Activity Pages
    Animal prints   81
    Aquifer   47
    Arrowheads   35
    Building Blocks for a Cave   14
    Cracking ice   22
    Creating a Caldera   39
    Finding Your Pulse   13
    Playing in the Mud   96
    Water Weir   50
    Wildflower seeds   70
Angel's Window   24
Animals & Wildlife   71
Aqua Fria River   58
Aquifer   47
Arches & Bridges   20

Ball court, Wupatki   88
Bats   12
Bill Williams River   58
Blow hole, Wupatki   88
Bonita Lava flow   34

Canyon point sinkhole   19
Caves   6
Colossal   17
Chiricahua Mountains   38
Colorado River   55, 61

Dams & Reclamation   58, 59
Devil's Bridge   25
Devil's Kitchen sinkhole   18

Ecological Zones   65
Ellison Creek   51

Fairbank   98
Fish Hatcheries   85
Fort Bowie   99

Fort Rucker   99
Fort Verde   99
Fossil Creek   47, 57

Gila River   58
Grand Canyon   60
Grand Canyon Caverns   16
Grand Canyon Deer Farm   73
Grand Falls   53
Green & Growing   64

Havasupai   48, 51
Historic Sites, 1800s era   96
Hoodoos   38, 40
Hot springs   55

Indian Gardens   60

Karchner Caverns   11, 13, 16
Keyhole Sink   53
Kinlichee   93

Lake Mead   62
Lake Pleasant   54
Lake Powell   62
Land of Standing Up Rocks   41
Lava River   17, 37
Limestone   41
Lonely Dell Ranch   97

Map Pages
    Arizona   9
    Caves   17
    Sinkholes   19
    Bridges & Arches 24
    Dams & Reservoirs   58
    Fish Hatcheries   85
    Homes in the 1800s   93
    Mines 29

National Parks   99
Native American Ruins   92
Native Tribe Reservations   97
Petroglyphs   87
Sand Dunes   40
Swimming Holes   56
State Parks   101
Volcanoes   40
Waterfalls   53
Marble Canyon   62
Mines   26
Mooney Falls   51
Mount Elden   33
Mount Humphries   32

National Parks   99
Native American Ruins   86
    Apache Brush House   88
    Besh Ba Gowah   95
    Betatkin   89, 95
    Hogan   89
    Kinlichee   95
    Palatki 7 / Verde Valley ruins   94
    Pit house   88
    Tonto Cliff Dwellings   94
    Walnut Canyon   94
    White House   95
    Wupatki   88, 90, 91, 94
Native Tribes map   93

Old Caves Crater   36

Painted Rocks   86
Paradise Forks   48
Petroglyphs   86
Phantom Ranch   60

Railroad Tunnel   30
Rainbow Bridge   24
Reservoirs   56, 58
Riparian zone   55
Robbers Roost   17
Roosevelt Lake   51

Salt, Gila, Verde and other Rivers 58

Sabino Canyon / Bear Canyon   52
Sand dunes   42
Sandstone   42
San Francisco Peaks   31
Seven Falls   52
Sierra Anchas   51
Sinkhole   18
Slide Rock Arch   25
Slime (algae)   70
Slot, Antelope slot   63
Snow   44
Spelunking   15
Springs   45, 55
Stalachtites & stalagmites   10
State Parks   100
Sunset Crater   32, 36
Swimming holes   56
Sycamore Falls   48

Tinaja   46
Tips for saving water   52
Tombstone   99
Tonto Cliff Dwellings   93
Tonto Natural Bridge   20
Travertine   20
Tubac & Tumacacori   96

Vegetation (Green & Growing)   64
Verde River   51, 58
Volcanoes   31
Vultee Arch   25

Water   44
Waterfalls   47
Water Safety tips   57
Water weir   50
Wave cave   17
White House ruin   93
White Mesa Arch   25
Wildflowers   69
Windowrock Arch   25
Windsor Castle   96
Workman Creek Falls   48

Yuma Territorial Prison   97

www.ingramcontent.com/pod-product-compliance
Lightning Source LLC
Chambersburg PA
CBHW041441010526
44118CB00003B/143